PETTICOATS AND WHITE FEATHERS

Recent Titles in
Contributions in Women's Studies

PETTICOATS AND WHITE FEATHERS

Gender Conformity, Race,
the Progressive Peace
Movement, and the Debate
Over War, 1895–1919

Erika A. Kuhlman

D
639
,P77
K84
1997
West

Contributions in Women's Studies, Number 160

GREENWOOD PRESS
Westport, Connecticut • London

Library of Congress Cataloging-in-Publication Data

Kuhlman, Erika A., 1961–
  Petticoats and white feathers : gender conformity, race, the
progressive peace movement, and the debate over War, 1895–1919 /
Erika A. Kuhlman.
      p.   cm. — (Contributions in women's studies, ISSN 0147–104X
; no. 160)
    Includes bibliographical references and index.
    ISBN 0–313–30341–X (alk. paper)
    1. World War, 1914–1918—Protest movements—United States.
2. World War, 1939–1945—Women—United States. 3. Feminists—United
States—Political activity. 4. Peace movements—United States—
History—20th century. 5. Progressivism (United States politics)
6. United States—Politics and government—1913–1921. I. Title.
II. Series.
D639.P77K84   1997
940.3'16—DC21   97–2225

British Library Cataloguing in Publication Data is available.

Library of Congress Catalog Card Number: 97 2225
ISBN: 0–313–30341–X
ISSN: 0147–104X

First published in 1997

Greenwood Press, 88 Post Road West, Westport, CT 06881
An imprint of Greenwood Publishing Group, Inc.

Printed in the United States of America

The paper used in this book complies with the
Permanent Paper Standard issued by the National
Information Standards Organization (Z39.48–1984).

10 9 8 7 6 5 4 3 2 1

Copyright Acknowledgment

The author and publisher gratefully acknowledge the Swarthmore College Peace Collection for permission to quote from the following archival sources as cited in the text: Records of the American Union Against Militarism; Records of the Emergency Peace Federation; Records of the Woman's Peace Party; and Records of the World Peace Foundation.

For my parents, Paul Kuhlman and Dolores Kuhlman,
and my sister, Rebecca Kuhlman

Contents

Figures

Preface

This book developed out of my experiences during the period of the Persian Gulf War. On January 13, 1991, the U.S. Congress voted to approve the use of force against the Iraqi dictator Saddam Hussein. President George Bush sent troops to conduct an air war on January 19. At the time, I was an instructor in humanities at the University of Montana in Missoula. As events surrounding the only "official" war to occur during my adulthood unfolded, I watched as many Missoulians mobilized themselves and others into action.

Decades earlier, another Montanan, Representative Jeannette Rankin, declared that the United States would be better served if it developed the "habit of peace." My colleagues in the University of Montana Humanities Department, especially Michael Kreisberg, Phil Fandozzi, Paul Dietrich, and Roger Dunsmore, had developed those habits: they knew precisely what to do in the face of the war. They cancelled our weekly humanities lecture and instead held a forum on the war, inviting special speakers but also allowing time for students and teachers to voice their attitudes, opinions, and fears regarding the war. Later, when a draft appeared possible, others in the university community scheduled a workshop on conscientious objection. I realized that much of the impetus behind the flurry of activity was older Missoulians' experiences as protesters during the Vietnam War. Seeing firsthand what Rankin meant by "habits of peace" eventually led to this study.

I wish to thank Michael Kreisberg and Bob Cushman in Missoula for helping me reconstruct events during the Gulf War. At Washington State University, professors LeRoy Ashby, Noël Sturgeon, Susan Armitage, and T. V. Reed were my mentors. Ashby provided me with infinite editorial and intellectual guidance. Sturgeon whispered a tantalizing suggestion that stuck with me — that I could revise the manuscript and send it to a publisher. Reed gave me input and encouragement in the earliest stages of this project, when I benefited greatly from his American Studies seminar. Armitage patiently guided me through a first draft. At Idaho State University, Dan Rylance brought new excitement to this project with his knowledge of and experience with the newspaper business and Congress, and with his editorial expertise. Peter Boag, Bob Swanson, and Ron Hatzenbuehler drew my attention to important scholarship along the way. Thanks also to editors at Greenwood.

Research for this book began with a grant from the Washington State University History Department. Every peace historian's dream come true, the Swarthmore College Peace Collection helped with illustrations and loaned microfilm. The Montana Historical Society made its Rankin Collection available to me. Tony Pisani at the Museum of the City of New York helped with photographs of World War I posters. Kevin Marsh provided needed companionship and last-minute legwork. To many others who expressed the excitement and encouragement that kept me going through the writing of this book, I offer my sincere gratitude.

1

Mustering Support for War:
Gender, Culture, and Language

During World War I, belligerent nations lured hesitant young men into military service by appealing to their sense of manhood. To illustrate this point in her feminist, pacifist journal, *Four Lights*, editor Sarah N. Cleghorn used a picture of a card and white feather that had been sent to a young Canadian man who refused to enlist in the military, an act for which he paid "the penalty of the White Feather." The card read, "Wanted: Petticoats for all able-bodied men who prefer staying at home when their country needs them." A woman who secured the enlistment of ten young men, reported Cleghorn, received a brooch for her efforts. "It is of such conditions," she concluded, "that the new courage is being born." During World War I, white feathers came to symbolize "effeminate" Canadian, American, and British men who refused to join the armed forces. Interestingly, according to some writers, it was female patriots — not soldierly doughboys — who paraded through city streets distributing white feathers to male bystanders not in uniform.[1]

But both sexes used the tactic of linking pacifism and resistance to the military with womanly accessories such as petticoats, to ridicule gender deviance, reward gender conformity, and win converts to war. Conventional images of weak, vulnerable femininity and strong, protective masculinity reverberated throughout all levels of American society on the eve of the war: in the halls of Congress, within the pages of the press, among circles of progressive reformers, and even among pacifists who earlier had recorded their fundamental opposition to war.

During the Progressive Era, Americans both adapted to and resisted a complex modernizing and industrializing society. Changing gender roles and identities produced widespread anxiety among men and women, an uneasiness that intensified as the nation began preparing for military combat. Concomitantly, the power of the progressive class (see Chapter 2 for discussion of progressives as a class rather than a political group) — whose members mediated these changes in American society — became entrenched. Pacifists, and the submovement within progressivism that they created, also reached a zenith of popularity as the debate over war raged. How can historians explain expanding involvement in the peace movement just as pressure began building to join the European war? Ironically, some antiwar reformers not only accepted intervention but even applauded it. Why and how did so many progressive pacifists end up forming one of the most vocal factions supporting U.S. intervention in World War I?

The study that follows is a history of the formation of the progressive class and the role progressive pacifists played in the decision to prepare for, and ultimately to intervene in, the Great War. More particularly, it is a history of how concepts of masculinity and femininity, and their relations to notions of militarism, democracy, citizenship, and race, became the most important factor (though not the only factor) in the creation of public and government endorsement of U.S. intervention in World War I.

But support for war, though seemingly ubiquitous, was not monolithic or static. My interest in this subject originated in the perception that although most progressive Americans ultimately registered consent to the decision to enter the war, continued resistance dampened the spirited pro-war atmosphere: indeed, President Woodrow Wilson outlined how he would deal with dissenters in his War Message delivered before Congress voted for war.[2] It seemed clear to me that rehearing both sides of the debate would help sort out how interventionists created support for war and how and why nay-sayers continued to protest. The dialectic relationship between the two sides is the real subject of this study.

Conventional periodization of the American past contributed to the perception that resistance to the war was insignificant. According to many historians of progressivism, U.S. entry into World War I helped to smother the reform spirit, which ultimately proved vulnerable to wartime mobilization and to the repressive laws designed to weed out those who did not support the government's war effort.[3] Certainly the progressives' enthusiasm for education and science led them to believe that the human ability to reason had evolved beyond the need to resort to combat: Jane Addams expressed her "astonishment that such an archaic institution should be revived in Modern Europe," and Emily Greene Balch considered war "as obsolete as chain armor."[4] The decision by Congress to enter the war ended their naiveté. But some progressive pacifists did not give up their active resistance as a result of the congressional vote: historians who conceive of the war as an end of one era and the beginning of another do protesters a disservice. A teleological approach to the debate over World War I depicts the public as mindlessly following the lead of the president, thereby painting a false picture of compliancy among the American public, one that does not explain continued resistance.

The question of how and why a nation declares war is further obscured by historians' inattention to the congressional debate within their discussions of American intervention. Many accounts of the peace movement give only a few lines to the debate in Congress over Wilson's War Message. In glossing the presidential speech, they also ignore pacifists' attempts to influence Congress and the twelve hours lawmakers spent formulating responses to the president's request. When historians merely record the war declaration without offering an analysis of the content of the debate over the declaration, they presume that what Congress or the public may have said did not matter, that the war was simply meant to be, an irrevocable consequence of human nature.[5]

This study uses a theoretical framework to historicize the debate over U.S. entry into the First World War. It draws upon social and linguistic theories to analyze the formation of the white progressive class, the creation of a progressive pacifist ideology, and the use of progressive ideology to justify U.S. intervention in the conflict. Concomitantly, it analyzes the feminist, pacifist challenge to intervention and to the gendered and race-biased assumptions of progressivism itself. The strategy in choosing a framework to explore this historical context was to see the sources through a layered lens, each layer bringing both pro-war and antiwar forces into clearer and clearer focus. For example, notions of what constitutes proper masculine and feminine behavior and what role each sex should play in society help create and reinforce social hierarchies: race operates alongside gender in much the same way. Using a concept such as cultural hegemony provides a way of viewing history as a series of attempts by the dominant social group to obtain consent to unpopular policies, such as war, from the rest of society. This approach differs from a teleological narrative, where "a nation" progresses toward a predetermined destiny. One way the dominant social group achieves consent is through the language it uses to promote its ideology. The linguistic theories of the twentieth-century Russian literary critic Mikhail Bakhtin allow for a closer analysis of how language acts as a power distributor. Each of the three analytical tools used in this study — gender and race, cultural hegemony, and language — is explained below.

GENDER, RACE, AND HISTORY

After winning suffrage, Montana's women voters helped send the nation's first female representative, antiwar campaigner and suffragist Jeannette Rankin, to Congress in 1916, shortly before both the war declaration and the final passage of the national suffrage amendment. Rankin could not have arrived in Washington at a more serendipitous moment, both for pacifists and suffragists. But her election produced other important consequences as well. For Rankin's male colleagues, seeing a woman in their midst who was handling reporters' questions, answering constituents' mail, and receiving honors for her contributions to women's rights, reminded them of an important fact about life in the early twentieth century: women were entering positions previously closed to them and, in the case of Rankin, casting a vote equivalent to a man's. Judging by their evaluations of her performance in the House, her male coworkers watched her with a critical eye. Was she capable of handling the affairs of government in a logical, rational manner? Or would she allow her emotions to overwhelm her thought processes and dictate her decisions? Of more immediate importance on the night of the vote on President Wilson's war declaration, would she, wondered newspaper reporters, other congressmen, and her constituents in Montana, take her brother's advice and "vote a man's vote?"[6]

Ideas about what constitutes proper behavior for women and men help shape history and determine, in part, how historians write about the past. Congress was (and, to a lesser extent, still is) a male-centered institution where predominantly white men determined the direction of American history: historians themselves, through their narrative descriptions about "great men" creating a progressively more enlightened nation, also participated in male domination of American society and institutions. But in the 1970s, new ways of conceiving of the past disrupted this tradition. The new social history placed "ordinary people" on the historical center stage, documented with a bevy of "everyday" source material: letters, diaries, and other personal accounts. To help amplify the voices of illiterate and less literate Americans, quantitative historians turned to census data and other statistical records. Women were often among those less literate groups of people who left behind fewer written records than their male counterparts. Historians of women began plundering factual resources and "personal" documents, thereby putting female contributors to American politics and culture at the forefront of their scholarship. Suddenly, women joined this new history as historical actors.

But feminists pondered the function of women's history as a subfield within the discipline. Was the purpose merely to examine how women's experiences differed from men's? One would then expect a description of Jeannette Rankin's tenure in Congress in comparison to the "standard" or "normal" experiences of a male representative. Some feminist historians complained that such treatments serve only to marginalize women further from social and political power. In other words, in a traditional history, Jeannette Rankin would seem to be merely an oddity in the history of male lawmakers, or worse, an accident.

What is needed is a study of how masculinity and femininity have shaped American society, culture, and politics. Gender, as defined by the historian Joan Wallach Scott, constitutes a complex web of social relationships based on perceived differences between the sexes and is a primary way of establishing relationships of power. Scott describes the interrelated elements of using gender as a category of historical analysis: First, gender includes cultural symbols that represent multiple (and often contradictory) roles for men and women.[7] On the one hand, World War I propaganda posters depicted women as ethereal angels of liberty or as mothers sacrificing for their sons (see Figure 1.1); on the other hand, recruitment posters showed uniformed women as active participants in war (although, significantly, never in combat). White men, too, were featured in war propaganda posters. Suited businessmen who did not enlist were depicted as being on the sidelines — on the "homefront" — of the war, contrasted with decorated soldiers participating in a great historical event. Or, conversely, laborers were depicted as brawny men making weapons to help destroy the enemy (see Figure 1.2).[8]

Second, gender includes the normative concepts with which people interpret the meanings of the symbols. These interpretations attempt to limit and contain proper behavior and roles for each sex. "Normative" here means images of women and men that a culture deems "normal": for example, women depicted as mothers, and men as breadwinners, conventional roles that limited the possibilities for both sexes. Victorians created the doctrine of "separate spheres" — fixed roles for men and women that supposedly never intertwined — in an attempt to place a fictive order on an increasingly chaotic, modernizing world. The point of a gendered history, according to Scott, is to disrupt these binary opposites, to unmask them as strategies designed to keep women marginalized, and, above all,

FIGURE 1.1

Source: *Women! Help America's Sons Win the War*, World War I Liberty Bond Poster, C. 1918, R. H. Porteus, artist. Gift of John W. Campbell to the Museum of the City of New York.

FIGURE 1.2

Source: These Men Have Come Across, They Are at the Front Now, World War I Navy Poster, C. 1917, Francis X. Leyendecker, artist. Gift of John W. Campbell to the Museum of the City of New York.

to avoid reinscribing them as "normal" and "natural."[9] A gendered interpretation of Jeannette Rankin, and other women like her, would explore how her powerful position challenged male and female complacency about men's traditionally dominant role in society. Rankin's male co-workers, of course, often became protective of their authority in response to female challenges. The beauty of using a gendered approach is that it enables historians to write about women without marginalizing them.

Recently, the historians Gail Bederman and Ann Douglas have demonstrated that gender ideologies often worked hand in hand with notions of racial supremacy. At the turn of the century, men explained male supremacy in terms of gender differences and also in terms of white racial dominance. Some progressive men claimed white male superiority both as an antidote to a culture that had grown lazy and effete and to protect an Anglo-dominated society threatened by massive African American migration to Northern cities and by immigration from Southern and Eastern Europe and Asia. To complicate matters further, progressive men differed in their responses to perceived racial threats. According to Bederman, some advocated renewed physical and spiritual energy to strengthen white manhood: others emphasized "reason" over "emotion," which they conflated with white "civilization" and nonwhite "savagery," respectively.[10]

Using gender as an analytic category also reveals how concepts of femininity depicted various factions within women's-rights movements. For even as one of the symbols of modernity — the "New Woman" of the post-Victorian era — stepped on stage, women (and men) disagreed on what part she should play. Feminists created different notions of proper gender roles and different strategies for combating male dominance. For example, some women in the national Woman's Peace Party (WPP) based their feminist pacifism on their perceptions of how women differed from men. The historian Linda Kay Schott, drawing on the psychologist Carol Gilligan's work *In a Different Voice* (1982), emphasized this feminist strategy within the WPP. What drove women to form a separate pacifist organization was, in part, their moral opposition to war. They sensed that "nothing was more important than the preservation of human life, that each individual deserved the best quality of life, and that conflicts could and must be solved without severing relationships between individuals or countries." But the strategy of arguing that women are different from men, which feminist theorists term "essentialism," proved problematic.[11] Once interventionists began arguing for war as a way to shore up male-dominated democracy, the WPP brand of feminist pacifism — based on morality as an exclusively female trait — was too easily dismissed as irrelevant to the debate over war.

CULTURAL HEGEMONY AND THE PRO-WAR VOTE

Jeannette Rankin cast her vote against war alongside 422 other lawmakers sitting in the House chambers. Fifty of the representatives rejected war, while 373 favored the declaration. In the Senate, the margin for war was greater: 82 to 6. Pacifists lobbied hard in the few days leading up to the vote, asking Congress to pass legislation enabling citizens to determine the question themselves. Many historians, including those sympathetic to Wilson, admitted that, indeed, a popular referendum might have gone against the president. The historian T. J. Jackson Lears pointed to the discrepancy between popular sentiment and the overwhelming pro-war vote in Congress and wondered why so many lawmakers ignored their constituents and voted with the president. Too frequently, noted Lears, public policy discussions, such as the debate over war, are treated as separate from private sentiment, implying that constituents do not — and cannot — influence government decision making. What was the interplay, wondered Lears, between the "official" discussion that resulted in war, and people's "private" musings? How were certain voices — both in 1917 and in historians' accounts of the war declaration — excluded from the debate and from historical descriptions of it?

Lears suggested that the Italian political theorist Antonio Gramsci's idea of cultural hegemony may shed light on this question, and on other problems, in American history.[12] I will not attempt to convey all of Gramsci's voluminous translated writings in this chapter, but I will explain four elements central to the concept of cultural hegemony — democratic groups, ideology, consent, and contradictory consciousness — that are useful in exploring the nuances and complexities of the decision to enter the Great War.

Writing in Italy in the 1920s, Antonio Gramsci developed a model of society used by cultural historians and political theorists to analyze the way culture influences the acquisition and distribution of power in capitalistic, democratic societies. By clarifying relationships of power between society's dominant and subordinate groups, Gramsci's model of cultural hegemony can help historians explain how the prevailing group uses culture — including the beliefs, values, prejudices, and norms that are embodied in cultural symbols — to define and reinforce its power.

DEMOCRATIC GROUPS

How do ruling classes gain hegemony? According to Gramsci, when ruling classes move beyond the economic interests of their own class and seek alliances with other social groups they become hegemonic. Progressives in government bureaucracies, for example, created alliances with organized labor and industry that resulted in "business unionism." Gramsci referred to subordinate groups — such as organized labor in the United States — as "democratic groups," by which he meant the social groups striving to obtain a legitimate voice within the existing power structure. Political advocates of such causes as suffrage and peace, which are not directly tied to economic productivity, also fall into this category. Most democratic groups do not seek to overturn the government or fundamentally to change the economic system. Some groups, indeed, in seeking greater power, may actually participate in maintaining and legitimating their own victimization (some labor historians argue that this occurred when labor merged more closely with business). At other times, however, democratic groups may work against the established class hegemony or indeed achieve hegemony themselves. The system of cultural hegemony, in other words, is fluid and open; the dissent of subordinate groups is permitted (except during war), creating a permeable barrier between the dominant and subordinate classes.

IDEOLOGY

Although Gramsci was a dedicated Marxist-Leninist, he detached Marxist thought from economic determinism. He adhered to Marx's base-superstructure model but widened the definition of "superstructure" to include civil society, made up of religious, educational, and political institutions. All these sectors of society participate in creating an ideology — or "a unity of faith between a conception of the world and a corresponding norm of conduct"[13] — with which the dominant class maintains its power and to which the subordinate class grants its consent. Cultural hegemony is thus both an explanation of how a ruling class attains its position in society (through obtaining the consent of the masses) and of how it maintains its power (through building up a broad bloc of varied social forces, unifed by an ideology).

THE PUBLIC'S CONSENT TO WAR

"Consent," however, is another ambiguous term within Gramsci's thought. In the twentieth century, democracies rule by means of a legal procedure; eligible voters grant authority to those they elect into office and in an "open" society voters may discuss and criticize what policies and laws the government institutes. But for Gramsci, consent is more complex than a legal procedure. Citizens become attached to, and agree with, certain core elements of the society. In a time of crisis, such as war, they may not agree with what their government does, but they give their consent nonetheless. For example, the antisuffragist Alice Hill Chittenden explained women's patriotic behavior during World War I as "service to the state," which she said was comparable to service to the family, "unselfish, unconditional, and unremitting." Chittenden regarded the government's request for service (in her view, a *gendered* notion of service) during a wartime crisis as legitimate.[14]

One of the ways the dominant class obtains the consent of the public is through manipulation of the press. Gramsci knew that the modern press began through technological innovations in communications, such as the telegraph, radio, and improved methods of printing, all of which required large sums of capital investment. Thus was born an intertwining of the interests of capital and those of the press. During a war, the press and the government work in conjuction to garner support for policies. "The State," wrote Gramsci, "when it wants to initiate an unpopular action or policy, creates in advance a suitable, or appropriate, public opinion; that is, it organizes and centralizes certain elements of civil society." As Gramsci described it, newspapers functioned as a pro-war lobby during World War I, achieving power and status equivalent to those of political parties.

The U.S. press functioned similarly during the war. Newspapers printed an outline of President Wilson's War Message, accompanied by favorable comments on the speech, *before* the actual vote that would involve the nation in war. Six days before Congress debated the war declaration, the *Washington Post* assured its readers that "Congress [stood] Firm Behind Wilson." The *New York Times* simply reported, "It is to be war with Germany," which followed the headline "[congressional] Members Pleased by Decisive Stand the President Is to Take." The effect was to make it seem as though the speech would result in war, when in fact, war was still undeclared. By making the war seem "inevitable," newspapers helped take the debate over war out of the public's hands.[15]

CONTRADICTORY CONSCIOUSNESS

Gramsci suggested that at times the masses are totally disaffected from the ruling class, making consent impossible: this phenomenon he described as "contradictory consciousness." "Contradictory consciousness" means that what people accept as true (that the United States is a democracy, where people are free to speak) differs from what is happening around them (people thrown in jail for speaking against the president's war policies). This condition, Gramsci believed, accounted for the passive acceptance of a government's unpopular mandates.[16]

For as much as Gramsci freed Marxist doctrines from rigid dogmatism, however, his revolutionary ideology was itself teleological. That is, he assumed that the end product of the hegemony of the ruling class would be worker revolution. Given his dedication to the proletariat, he focused only on class differences. Although he mentioned women's-rights organizations as an example of a democratic group trying to wedge a foot in the door of power, he saw this attempt as futile: women would simply be incorporated, or absorbed, into the ruling class.[17]

Nevertheless, cultural hegemony remains a useful concept for historians of gender. Indeed, as a category of analysis, gender intersects a Gramscian class analysis. In the months before U.S. intervention, the pro-war camp, attempting to win support for belligerency, used gendered language to appeal to men across class boundaries, and therefore *against* women pacifists. Race worked the same way: when interventionists began using racist notions of "civilization" versus "barbarism," they appealed to white men and women, again, across class interests.

"BUY A BOND": LANGUAGE AS A PRO-WAR TOOL

One week after the war declaration passed Congress, President Wilson sought ways to muffle lingering dissent and ensure public compliance with wartime policies, such as the draft. He hired the progressive journalist George Creel to head a new bureaucracy, which he called the Committee on Public Information. Creel hired artists, writers, and actors to circulate propaganda for what he called "a national ideology" of patriotic, pro-war sentiment. The Committee on Public Information used powerful, gendered symbols, which were designed to appeal to men and women across class boundaries, in order to solidify support for war from all sectors of American society. Significantly, however, the men and women featured in propaganda posters were always white.[18]

White feathers, and other wartime symbols such as Uncle Sam, female figures representing liberty, and manly uniformed recruits, signified a unified language used to help "combat" dissent. At the same time, symbols of the enemy, such as the clenched fist of the "Hun," were devised to evoke hatred and a fighting fervor among viewers. Bakhtin developed theories of language useful in helping historians analyze the way words and symbols work in a society to create support for, or dissent from, public policies. Bakhtinian conceptualizations such as dialogism, heteroglossia, and tact, aid historians' analyses of the discursive practices employed by both those in favor of, and those opposed to, war, thereby creating a useful dialogue between the two sides.

Like Gramsci, Bakhtin viewed history as driven by the domination of different and unequal social classes, each fighting for political control over society. But Bakhtin placed primary emphasis on language, which he believed gave experience form and determined its direction. "Language becomes the space of confrontation of differently-oriented social accents," wrote the literary critic Robert Stam of Bakhtin's theories, "as diverse socio-linguistic consciousnesses fight it out on the terrain of language. While the dominant class strives to make language uni-accentual . . . the oppressed strive to deploy language for their own liberation."[19] Language, then, determines relationships of power in a society.

USING LANGUAGE TO ANALYZE
THE DEBATE OVER WAR

According to Bakhtin, all verbal expression takes place in the form of dialogue. Speech, or utterance, contains two parts: signification, which is the part of an utterance that can be reproduced (the actual words used by the speaker), and meaning, which depends on a number of factors, such as setting and the values of the speaker, which cannot always be reproduced. To understand how hegemonic groups maintain power, the language they adopt (for example, words and phrases such as "slacker" and "buy a bond" that became popular during World War I) must be considered in the context in which they appeared (in newspaper ads and posters designed to encourage people to support the war). The function of these popular phrases during wartime was to unify and centralize language. Bakhtin suggested that political power consists partly in the capacity to place one's terms in wide circulation, a tactic both Gramsci and Bakhtin recognized as crucial to obtaining the consent of the public.

HETEROGLOSSIA

Speech consists of individual speakers communicating to and anticipating responses from other speakers. Bakhtin used the term *heteroglossia* to mean the larger linguistic context of all social dialogues. Stam explained the same term as meaning different voices that represent distinct positions within a society and that are often in conflict with the larger society. Language, in other words, is competitive: different classes, races, and genders use language to gain a larger voice, and therefore more power, in society.[20]

Suffragists' discourse and that of the male voters they tried to convince illustrate the meaning of the term *heteroglossia*. According to Douglas, the suffragist leader Carrie Chapman Catt explained that women resented American men for enfranchising Negroes before American wives and mothers. In other words, Catt conflated nationality — "American" — with the white race when she argued that white men should value American — white — women before Negroes. Catt's argument was designed to convince Southern white supremacists to vote for woman suffrage. At the same time, suffrage advocates described potential Irish immigrant voters to Northern men in the same way, using the same strategies they had used in the South.[21]

POLYPHONY

Polyphony, another Bakhtinian term, seeks an escape from the constant contentiousness of heteroglossia. Polyphony differs from heteroglossia in that it means not simply recognizing diverse voices *but actually providing a context for difference*. Polyphony is harmonious, while heteroglossia is combative. With this concept, Gramsci and Bakhtin parted company. Gramsci believed that in a hegemonic system, opposing views in most cases are tolerated (except during war). But Bakhtin's notion of polyphony not only tolerates diversity; it actually encourages it. While Gramsci suggested that, for the most part, democratic groups are subsumed by the hegemonic class, Bakhtin staked out a conceptual space for them to exist and to be heard (i.e., not absorbed into the dominant social group).

MONOLOGUE

Bakhtin's term for the reverse of polyphony was *monologism*. Monologism describes those utterances that do not recognize a different point of view. Monologism "defies that there exists outside of it another consciousness, with the same rights, and capable of responding on equal footing, another equal [opinion]." According to Bakhtin, "The monologue is accomplished and deaf to the other's responses. Monologue makes do without the other; this is why, to some extent it objectifies all reality. Monologue pretends to be the last word."[22]

President Wilson's War Message is a good example of monologism. Wilson arrived at the Capitol, delivered his speech, and was escorted out; the setting allowed no forum for questions. The president was not preparing for a confrontation with those opposed to his plans. He recognized the existence of an opposition but then went on to describe what he would do to control dissenters. More conventional historic treatments of the speech and the congressional debate that followed mask the power relationships between the pro- and antiwar factions by either assuming there was little or no opposition — the historian Arthur Link mentions the debate in one paragraph — or by focusing on the opposition without attending to its relationship with the dominant group (David Thelen's work, *Robert M. La Follette and the Insurgent Spirit*, and John Milton Cooper, Jr.'s *The Vanity of Power* are notable exceptions).[23] A Bakhtinian reading of Wilson's speech teases out the voices of opposition stirring within it, while at the same time uncovering the ways the speech repressed opposition, thereby revealing the relationships of power between the two sides.

TACT

Bakhtin used the word *tact* to mean the role that context plays in the meaning of an utterance. To "hear" the meaning of an utterance fully, one must consider the circumstances under which it was delivered. Speech, in other words, does not occur apart from space and time. Attending to the tact of congressional debate reveals who in Congress had the authority to speak; whose voice inexperienced freshmen and women were likely to hear; and how rules, both formal and informal, shaped the debate.

"Tact" refers to the ensemble of codes governing interaction in discourse. The codes are determined by the aggregate of all speakers, their ideologies, and the circumstances of their conversation. When historians re-hear the 1917 congressional debate, they must consider not only the signification, or the part of the speech that can be reiterated, but also the setting, which is more difficult to reconstruct. Setting also includes those "invisible" constituents whose voices, though not literally present, are nonetheless alluded to from time to time in the congressional debate.

Debate in Congress is regulated by rules made by each house. These rules include the order in which members are allowed to speak and whether or not they can interrupt the speech of another to ask a question or make a point. All these rules restrict the debate of Congress and are crucial to a Bakhtinian analysis of the debate.

Bakhtin's notions of tact are useful in determining the degree to which debate in Congress allowed the voices of opposition to be heard. Freedom of speech is highly valued in a democracy, but how free were congressional representatives who opposed the president's war policies to make their views known? How persuasive did they sound? Did they articulate their own discourse, or were they unable to frame their arguments in any other language but that of the pro-war faction? In other words, how pluralistic (or polyphonic) was the 1917 debate over World War I? Bakhtin's theories complicate a part of history that has been told too simplistically. Many previous treatments view war as a natural human endeavor that neither Congress nor the public could hope to control; foreign policy is conducted by the president, and, during wartime, the president's decisions are not disputable. But a dialogic treatment of the process that sends a nation to war creates polyphony out of monologue, that is, in Bakhtinian terminology, the counterposing of two voices, pro- and antiwar, at a dialogical angle, transcends the individual content of the two discourses.

THE PUBLIC AND THE PRIVATE:
LANGUAGE AND RELATIONSHIPS
OF POWER BETWEEN MEN AND WOMEN

How can historians who are re-hearing the discursive practices of the past use what they hear "simultaneously [to] embrace . . . the public and the private — and the way meanings move back and forth between them?"[24] How can they use what they hear to discern relationships of power between men and women? The two propositions, in fact, are interrelated. Male domination is defined by female subordination, accomplished, in part, by keeping women's work "private." Feminists have turned to Bakhtin's notion of dialogism in order to break down this separation of public rationality and private intersubjectivity. The literary critics Dale M. Bauer and Susan Jaret McKinstry argue that "public" language attempts to reflect a neutral rationality and an impersonal authority, while "private" language is deemed improper for public or social issues.[25] During the congressional debate over war, representatives spoke of their private feelings on war but pushed them aside and voted rationally, "disinterestedly," for the sake of the nation.

Women and men define themselves in opposition to each other but also in relation to each other. Thus feminist linguists seek to include previously silenced voices in conversations about women. To what extent did women pacifists articulate their own discourse? Or did they remain trapped by that of their male counterparts?

Carroll Smith-Rosenberg uses Bakhtinian notions of language in her study of American women during the Victorian era. She contends that women did not adopt a male discourse; rather, they invested male images with female political intent. Women sought to use male myths to repudiate male power, to turn the male world upside down. Stam also explains the importance of discourse to political power: "A political opposition so completely trapped in the language of its enemy . . . has already lost half the battle." Smith-Rosenberg asks if embattled social and political groups survive when shorn of the power to create language. Or must such challengers use the language of the dominant groups in order to undermine them?[26]

In the chapters that follow, I have kept two questions in the forefront: First, How have notions of acceptable gender roles in American society influenced the evolution of the progressive peace movement? Second, How have those same notions been used to formulate a strategy, and a language, designed to gather support for war? Chapter 2 of this study describes the rise of the progressive class and of progressive pacifism. Progressives' experiences in the peace movement widened the boundaries of domestic reform to include the reform of relationships between nations. Concomitantly with their strategy of coalition building, progressive pacifists crafted their ideology of internationalism — the view that American-style democracy could and should form the basis of all the world's societies. But despite unified acceptance of ideology and tactic among progressive pacifists, divisions existed between and among progressive men and women. The rifts that developed reflected different perceptions of acceptable gender roles and different notions of femininity and masculinity.

Chapter 3 describes the formation of a hegemonic bloc among progressives in support of military preparedness. Begun by progressives seeking military reform, advocates of preparedness obtained the consent of progressive pacifists by formulating preparedness in the progressive terms of internationalism and by imbuing their rhetoric with gendered notions of manly strength and feminine vulnerability.

A similar pattern developed with regard to intervention. Chapter 4 describes how progressive interventionists promoted the war to reflect the progressive ideology of internationalism. Many female pacifists supported U.S. belligerency because they believed American intervention would help democratize the world and because they hoped their active consent to the war effort would win support for woman suffrage. Progressive male pacifists viewed U.S. participation as an opportunity to bolster what they perceived of as a sagging manhood and nationhood that they hoped war would reinvigorate. Most progressive men and women accepted American democracy as a male-dominated system that they were willing to fortify through intervention in the war. When Congress debated President Wilson's War Message, it did so using conventional notions of male supremacy, which some lawmakers promoted as *white* male superiority.

Chapter 5 examines a group of feminist pacifists who continued to protest U.S. participation in the war. The New York City Woman's Peace Party offered an alternative view of the war and of the society that supported militarism. Their gender-based criticism of American society and democracy ruptured the hegemony of the progressive class.

NOTES

1. Sarah N. Cleghorn, *Four Lights* (6 Feb 1917), SR reel 23.01 (hereafter abbreviated SR 23.01), Woman's Peace Party (hereafter abbreviated WPP) Papers, Swarthmore College Peace Collection (hereafter abbreviated SCPC); Sandra M. Gilbert, "Soldier's Heart: Literary Men, Literary Women, and the Great War," in *Behind the Lines: Gender and the Two World Wars*, ed. Margaret Randolph Higgonet et al. (New Haven: Yale University Press, 1987), 209; Helen M. Cooper, Adrienne Auslander Munich, and Susan Merrill Squier, eds., *Arms and the Woman: War, Gender, and Literary Representation* (Chapel Hill: University of North Carolina Press, 1989), xiii. For a fictional account of gender conformity among men with respect to war, see Katherine Anne Porter's short story "Pale Horse, Pale Rider," in *Pale Horse, Pale Rider*, 1936 (reprint, New York: Modern Library, 1939).

2. Susan Zeiger, "She Didn't Raise Her Boy to Be a Slacker: Motherhood, Conscription, and the Culture of the First World War," *Feminist Studies* 22 (Spring 1996): 7–39, argues that leaders of war mobilization took continued pacifist dissent seriously, turning feminist pacifist rhetoric against women protesters; Wilson's speech appears in the *Congressional Record*, 65th Congress, 1917, 120.

3. The exception to this periodization is Dorothy Schneider and Carl J. Schneider, *American Women in the Progressive Era, 1900–1920* (New York: Facts on File, 1992); Neil A. Wynn, *From Progressivism to Prosperity: World War I and American Society* (New York: Holmes and Meier, 1986); and Henry May, *The End of American Innocence: A Study of the First Years of Our Own*

Time, 1912–1917 (New York: Knopf, 1959), argues that progressivism was collapsing already, before U.S. intervention.

4.   Jane Addams quoted in *From Progressivism to Prosperity*, by Neil A. Wynn (New York: Holmes and Meier, 1988), 26; Mercedes M. Randall, *Improper Bostonian: Emily Greene Balch* (New York: Twayne, 1964), 134.

5.   The question of how the United States reached the decision to declare war in 1812 is explained in Ronald L. Hatzenbuehler and Robert L. Ivie, *Congress Declares War: Rhetoric, Leadership, and Partisanship in the Early Republic* (Kent, Ohio: Kent State University Press, 1983).

6.   Quoted in *Flight of the Dove: The Story of Jeannette Rankin*, by Kevin S. Giles (Beaverton, Ore.: Touchstone Press, 1980), 90. According to Giles, newspapers sensationalized Rankin's behavior when she voted against the declaration. See, for example, the article under the headline, "Only Woman in Congress Collapses as She Decides," *New York Times*, 7 April 1917, 1.

7.   Joan Wallach Scott, *Gender and the Politics of History* (New York: Columbia University Press, 1988), 42–43.

8.   See Walton Rawls, *Wake Up, America! World War I and the American Poster* (New York: Abbeville Press, 1988), for reproductions of recruitment, Red Cross, Liberty Bond, and other war-related posters.

9.   Scott, *Gender and the Politics of History*, 43.

10.   Gail Bederman, *Manliness and Civilization: A Cultural History of Gender in the United States, 1880–1917* (Chicago: University of Chicago Press, 1995), 6–7, 11, 16–17; Ann Douglas, *Terrible Honesty: Mongrel Manhattan in the 1920s* (New York: Farrar, Straus, and Giroux, 1995), 258.

11.   Linda Kay Schott, "The Women's Peace Party and the Moral Basis for Women's Pacifism," *Frontiers* 7, no. 2 (1985): 20; Carol Gilligan, *In a Different Voice: Psychological Theory and Women's Development* (Cambridge: Harvard University Press, 1982); Joan C. Tronto discusses Gilligan's interpretations and essentialism in *Moral Boundaries: A Political Argument for an Ethic of Care* (New York: Routledge, 1993), 77–85.

12.   T. J. Jackson Lears, "The Concept of Cultural Hegemony: Problems and Possibilities," *American Historical Review* 90 (June 1985): 567–593.

13.   Antonio Gramsci, *Selections from the Prison Notebooks*, ed. and trans. Quintin Hoare and Geoffrey Nowell Smith (New York: International Publishers, 1971), 326.

14.   Quoted in *American Women's Activism in World War I*, by Barbara J. Steinson (New York: Garland Press, 1982), 317.

15.   Gramsci quoted in *Gramsci's Political Thought: Hegemony, Consciousness, and the Revolutionary Process*, by Joseph V. Femia (Oxfordshire: Clarendon Press, 1981), 27; Gramsci, *Selections from the Prison Notebooks*, 228; *Washington Post*, 31 March 1917, 1; *New York Times*, 31 March 1917, 1.

16.   Joseph V. Femia, *Gramsci's Political Thought: Hegemony, Consciousness, and the Revolutionary Process* (Oxfordshire: Clarendon Press, 1981), 43.

17.   Lears, "Cultural Hegemony," 578; Gramsci, *Selections from the Prison Notebooks*, 296. Gramsci did not write extensively on women.

18.   Zeiger, "She Didn't Raise Her Boy," treats the CPI and its wartime propaganda, especially in film; Wynn, *From Progressivism to Prosperity*, devotes a chapter to blacks in World War I (170–195); on pp. 48–49, he notes one film made by the CPI called *Our Colored Fighters*.

19.   Robert Stam, "Mikhail Bakhtin and Left Cultural Critique" in *Postmodernism and its Discontents*, ed. E. Ann Kaplan (London: Verso, 1988), 116–145.

20.   Ibid.

21.   Douglas, *Terrible Honesty*, 258; Aileen Kraditor, *The Ideas of the Woman Suffrage Movement, 1890–1920* (New York: Columbia University Press, 1965) delves into the suffragists' strategies. Margaret Deland describes attitudes toward Irish immigrant voters (utilizing the euphemisms "Patrick" and "Bridget"). See Deland, "The Change in the Feminine Ideal," *Atlantic Monthly* 105 (March 1910): 289–302.

22.   Bakhtin quoted in *Mikhail Bakhtin: The Dialogic Principle*, by Tzvetan Todorov, trans. Wlad Godzich (Minneapolis: University of Minnesota Press, 1984), 107.

23.   Arthur S. Link, *Woodrow Wilson: Campaigns for Peace and Progressivism, 1916–1917* (Princeton: Princeton University Press, 1965) describes the setting of Wilson's speech on 423; Arthur S. Link, *Woodrow Wilson and the Progressive Era, 1910–1917* (New York: Harper, 1954), 281–282; David P. Thelen, *Robert M. La Follette and the Insurgent Spirit* (Boston: Little, Brown and Co., 1976); John Milton Cooper, Jr., *The Vanity of Power: American Isolationism and the First World War, 1914–1917* (Westport, Conn.: Greenwood Press, 1969).

24.   Thomas Bender, quoted in Lears, "Cultural Hegemony," 586.

25.   Dale M. Bauer and Susan Jaret McKinstry, eds. *Feminism, Bakhtin and the Dialogic* (New York: State University of New York Press, 1991), 2.

26.   Carroll Smith-Rosenberg, "Writing History: Language, Class, and Gender," in *Feminist Studies — Critical Studies*, ed. Teresa D'Lauretis (Bloomington: University of Indiana Press, 1986), 31–54; Stam, "Mikhail Bakhtin," 124.

2

"To Re-Educate the World": The Origins and Ideology of the Progressive Peace Movement

Men and women living from 1895 to 1919 witnessed profound upheavals in American society, caused by massive industrialization, rapid urban growth, large-scale immigration, and the rise of the corporation. Middle-class reformers tackled these problems with an unprecedented combination of vigorous energy and a confident — if naive — sense of optimism. Progressivism generated a complex blend of social criticism, economic and political restructuring and regulation, and social-welfare legislation. Progressive reformers organized around issues of labor unrest, moral reform, conservation of resources, and international conflict. In some cases, government bureaucracies, such as the U.S. Children's Bureau, were formed in response to progressive efforts. Progressivism, according to the historian John A. Thompson, was "marked by a particular 'mood,' 'temper,' or 'ethos' — one sympathetic to calls for reform."[1] But progressives were never in complete harmony on all issues or even on the meanings or implications of the movement they formed. Historians have asked a series of questions in their search for meaning and synthesis of the Progressive Era: Was progressivism an essentially liberal or a fundamentally conservative movement? Were its advocates the elitist men of a bygone era, desiring to recapture political power in a democratizing nation, or were the progressives themselves democrats, attempting to diffuse political and social power among an educable populace? Did the movement spawn cultural diversity or homogeneity?[2]

Progressive reformers formed an economic group, a new middle class, which became hegemonic as they captured and maintained power through an ideology expressed in a popular, unified language. Furthermore, they broadened their base of support by creating alliances among various political-interest groups. Within the progressive class, progressive pacifists developed an ideology of apparent internationalism, that in fact rested on the assumed superiority of American democracy relative to other nations, and a code of behavior, the building of coalitions among groups with diverse interests, with which they attempted to control American society. Three pacifist groups — the World Peace Foundation (WPF), the Woman's Peace Party (WPP), and the American Union Against Militarism (AUAM) — each embraced progressive pacifist ideology. Peace reformers, however, were never completely united on such questions as the nature of American democracy, the proper place of women in society, whether or not immigrants could be "Americanized," or, ultimately, whether or not the United States should enter the European war.

The history of the Progressive Era has evolved through a number of interpretive shifts. Coming from within the movement itself, the historians Mary Beard, Charles Beard, and Vernon Parrington viewed history as a continuous confrontation between democracy and privileged men who used political power in their own interests. In the 1950s, Richard Hofstadter launched a revision of this paradigm. Rather than viewing American history as a battle between democracy and privilege, he saw industrial capitalism as a system to which all Americans gave their consent. His study of the progressives' economic and social background revealed that reformers represented a privileged class in a modern world that they could no longer control; progressivism developed out of their fear of losing established, elitist positions of authority in society. As the historian David Kennedy summed up Hofstadter's view, progressive reform was marked more by "a hankering for a more certain economic system in which individual moral character could be tested," than by any truly democratic impulse.[3]

New Left interpretations of progressivism returned to the older, dualistic paradigm of "people" versus "interests." Gabriel Kolko argued that progressivism was an essentially conservative movement that made no real efforts to change the existing distribution of wealth. The rise of corporate capitalism should have produced a revolt by the people, but there were no major groups representing the underprivileged. (James Weinstein argued that the Socialist Party of America spoke for this group.) Progressivism, according to Kolko, only created the political means to achieve capitalists' ends: maintain the system of free enterprise, with enough regulation to socialize the country gently, but to thwart any real efforts at reform. For example, early on in the movement progressives did attempt fundamental changes: but after 1900, reformers accepted and tried simply to provide some checks on corporations, while the government accommodated large-scale business organizations and their methods.[4]

In the late 1960s, the dualistic model was once again overturned. Robert Wiebe drew from both Hofstadter and the New Left in his work, *The Search for Order: 1877–1920*. Wiebe, too, examined the backgrounds and motives of progressives, but his findings differed from Hofstadter's. Wiebe maintained that progressives represented a new middle class of ambitious, professional bureaucrats, not an anxiety-ridden, old-guard elite. A new class of experts succeeded in bringing system and rational order to a society suffering from disorder and inefficiency. Where Hofstadter found an irrational fear of loss of status, Wiebe found a rational group of scientific experts ready to create a new middle class that would define society and culture by adapting Americans to a new mode of economic production: industrialization.[5]

John Buenker lent credence to the "order" school's interpretation by exploring the means by which the progressives achieved order. No single progressive interest group — for example, urban reformers — could hope to get favorable legislation passed on its own. To make up for their lack of numbers, groups formed alliances with other progressives of similar (at times, even dissimilar) interests. For example, housing reformers allied with health authorities to attack substandard housing as disease infested and dangerous to all city dwellers. This coalition-building strategy, according to Buenker, distinguishes the Progressive Era from other periods of reform in U.S. history.[6]

A different study of progressivism's intellectual underpinnings added to the dualistic model of progressive historiography. In the mid-1970s, James P. Martin explored the Darwinist foundations of progressive thought. All progressives, according to Martin, accepted the notion of struggle and competition, but they disagreed as to the limits of its application to society. On the one hand, Spencerian Darwinists were confident that struggle resulted in the best rising to the top; *if* society's experts educated the unenlightened, social betterment would result. Reform Darwinists, on the other hand, wanted to check the political power wielded by society's privileged by extending democracy to the poor and oppressed. Significantly, neither kind of progressive sought to abolish private property or capitalism; the reform division lay within the question of where political power should be located. Progressives shared common attitudes, however. Martin identified trust in human reason, belief in education to eradicate social problems, a sense of optimism, faith in the United States' mission to spread democracy, and, of course, belief in progress, which spawned the movement's name. These constituted the traditional American values that progressives feared losing in a modernizing, industrial world.[7]

Historians of women have more recently added new evidence and rich, fresh interpretations of women reformers during the Progressive Era. Progressive reform effected the breakdown of the doctrine of "separate spheres," according to Nancy S. Dye. In a modern, industrial society, "home and the community were inextricably bound together, and those concerns once defined as the private responsibility of individual housewives and mothers were actually public, and political." Contradictions within the separate-sphere ideology weakened its hold on women; while they were supposed to protect their households, the safety of children in large cities where anonymous forces, such as fast-moving street cars and large food-processing plants, seemed increasingly out of individual women's control. Women reformers sought to regain influence in urban areas and protect the home from the forces of the market. Many women's reform efforts explored and documented the connections between the private world of households and the political and economic institutions of the larger society.[8]

THE PROGRESSIVE CLASS

With the aid of linguistic and cultural theories, historians can begin to move toward a more nuanced analysis of progressivism, which includes elements from both the dualistic ("people" versus "interests") model and Wiebe's "order" interpretation. Antonio Gramsci's model of the formation of a hegemonic class provides a useful paradigm for rethinking historical analyses and interpretations, as well as progressivism itself. The first step (already taken by Wiebe) is to look at the progressives as a social class seeking power, rather than solely as a collection of men and women with similar political temperament and goals.

Gramsci broadened the definition of "social class" to include elements of a society's culture. For Gramsci, class was not limited to how a social group related to the means of production, or the economy. A class designation also meant how a group of people constructed their identity relative to other social groups and how that identity translated into a social structure. Many historians did not accept this definition of class, but some, such as Wiebe, understood progressivism as a class because they thought of class as a complex exchange between economic forces and cultural identity. According to the sociologist Anthony Giddens, studying class required an examination of "the modes in which 'economic' relationships become translated into 'non-economic' social structures."[9]

The years 1895 to 1919 can be understood as a time when women and men reformed their senses of self in response to drastic changes in the economic and institutional transformations that occurred as part of the process of industrialization. Historians call this period the Progressive Era because progressives achieved hegemony at a time when the United States' industrial economic base expanded rapidly. The old nineteenth-century social order was dying out; progressivism, as Wiebe pointed out, was an attempt by the new middle class to make itself into a distinctive class, by replacing old values with new ones better suited to changing economic and social conditions. One indication of this change occurred in how people constructed their identity: by their profession, rather than by the community in which they lived. Wiebe described how occupations, such as social work, became professions: first social workers organized and defined themselves by forming professional associations and then by requiring specific academic training. This process, as it applied to every profession from architecture to history, created a common bond among members of the new middle class.[10]

PROGRESSIVE IDEOLOGY

Hegemonic classes, according to Gramsci, vied for dominance in a world of conflicting ideologies. Progressives, as the New Left historians maintained, created a political atmosphere that both reformed and maintained the capitalist order. But the progressive class did more than merely synthesize economic and political aims; they also attempted to create intellectual and moral unity by developing a cultural and moral imperative. By developing an ideology, or "a unity of faith between a conception of the world and a corresponding norm of conduct,"[11] the progressive class dominated American society and culture. Progressivism, then, was an ideology, a way of looking at the world, with a corresponding mode of conduct: coalition building.

PROGRESSIVE DISCOURSE: CIVILIZATION, EFFICIENCY, EXPERTISE, AND PROFESSIONALISM

One way progressives achieved power was through the development of a distinctive discourse. As this new class achieved political and social dominance, it imposed cultural and linguistic hegemony over society.

Among the maxims of progressive discourse were terms such as *civiliza-tion*, *efficiency*, *expertise*, and *professionalism*. Taken together, these concepts formed the power base of the progressive class's ideology.

After the 1898 Spanish-American War, the United States became a colonial power in competition with European nations for control of the world's resources. One of the guiding ideologies of imperialism was the notion of "civilization," which imperialists contrasted with "barbarity." In support of their ideology of the *progress* of civilization versus the stagnant backwardness of savagery, progressives attempted to place a fictive order on a changing world. But, as Gail Bederman has shown, ideologies are complex. On the one hand, progressive men and women viewed the American white, middle class as more evolved than the "backward" races. The progressive pacifist David Starr Jordan, for example, worried that the Great War would result in the degeneration of the white race; the war was "working havoc without parallel in the best racial elements in all nations concerned, thereby exhausting the near future and bringing subsequent impoverishment, physical and mental, to the race." On the other hand, some progressives believed that American society was becoming *too* civilized. After the war began in Europe, the progressive pacifist Paul Kellogg counseled Americans to "do more than sit back to care for our own inter-ests, to grow fat and comfortable while the whole world is in agony." In other words, progressives hoped that action — and, ultimately, military action — would shake Americans' inertia.[12]

Progressives' interest in the social sciences and their faith in humans' ability to reason spawned an efficiency craze, which the historian Samuel Haber called the "secular great awakening." In economics, efficiency signaled an effective operation as measured by a comparison of produc-tion with cost. In physics, the term denoted the ratio of energy delivered by a system to the energy with which that system was supplied. Progres-sives applied this scientific term to human society: a government bureau-crat, for example, might calculate the cost of public education for immigrants based on immigrant productivity in the work force. Used in relation to individuals, efficiency meant an attitude: the valuing of reason over emotion, disciplined education over innate talent, and masculinity over femininity. In a collective sense, efficiency signified a harmonious relationship among men who accepted the leadership of professionals. Optimum efficiency required the expertise of college-educated men who led the masses in the interests of social harmony. Experts were men with empirically proven knowledge who, because they were supposedly free from class or political bias, theoretically worked for the betterment of mankind. However, according to Haber, "Efficiency provided a standpoint from which those [progressives] who had declared allegiance to democracy could resist the leveling tendencies of the principle of equality."[13]

Just as contradiction and controversy riddled the progressive concept of civilization, such was also true for efficiency, expertise, and professionalism. For example, Jane Addams, notable progressive reformer, disagreed with the privileged status most progressives granted to professionals. She saw professionalism as a force that thwarted spontaneity and direct emotional response: these, according to Addams, were the undercurrents of reform.[14] As the progressive peace movement sought linguistic and cultural hegemony, groups that were situated differently within the political and social power structure disagreed with progressive ideology and broke away to develop their own discourses.

Thus, progressivism was not totalitarian. Divisions developed between races, genders, ethnicities, and regions within this new class. Men and women, for example, experienced industrialism and the modern world differently from each other. They were situated differently within the power structure of society, as were people of different races. For example, progressives divided over the extent to which democracy should be granted to new immigrants, African Americans, and women. Many progressives were also elitist, trying to exclude certain people (the uneducated, those without expertise) from political power. Contradiction, as Carroll Smith-Rosenberg noted, lies at the heart of class identity.[15]

THE PROGRESSIVE PEACE MOVEMENT

As the historians C. Roland Marchand and James Parker Martin demonstrated, the American peace movement evolved as part of the progressive movement. Before the outbreak of war in 1914, pacifism, or the predisposition to oppose all war and to advocate the settlement of international conflict by peaceful means, became a popular reform among progressives. The peace movement reflected the tensions and the themes central to progressivism: the opposition of the "elite" to the popular will, the search for order and reason, the appeal of efficiency and expertise, and, most important, the uncertainty and anxiety produced by changing gender identities. Progressive pacifists developed a distinctive discourse and ideology (internationalism) and a code of behavior (coalition building), which they attempted to impose upon American society.

The progressive peace movement took shape in the mid-1890s. Beginning in 1895, a series of conferences on how international conflicts could be solved through arbitration, rather than by the use of force, was held at Lake Mohonk, New York. The Quakers Alfred and Daniel Smiley, proprietors of the resort hotel hosting the conference, hand picked the upper-class, genteel folk — churchmen, politicians, and scholars — who comprised the guest list. Alfred Smiley had decided that the time was ripe for an annual conference on international peace. Formerly a strict pacifist, he had recently been convinced by the Pullman strike and other labor problems that police and a militia were necessary for internal peace and stability. His main concern was promoting arbitration as a means of preventing violent outbreaks.[16]

Women, too, participated at the Lake Mohonk conferences. M. Carey Thomas, May Wright Sewell, and Lucia Ames Mead contended that they spoke from a woman's perspective; they believed war existed because American society relegated perceived feminine values to the private, domestic — rather than the public — sphere. But they foresaw the expansion of women's public role and predicted that women's activism would be based on the premise that the preservation and quality of human life and human relationships were contingent upon "the organizing skills of women." Female participants at Lake Mohonk, according to the historian C. F. Howlett, "sought a greater role for women in what was essentially a male-dominated peace movement." Within the next 20 years, women would get a chance to exercise those skills when Mead and others formed the Woman's Peace Party.[17]

After the Spanish-American War, American imperialism deeply disturbed almost all the Lake Mohonk participants. The peace movement became a vehicle for organizing American opinion against possible future imperialist ventures and against naval buildup. Responding to America's emergence as a major world power, those attending the conferences advocated treaties of international arbitration and mediation, and conciliation procedures, as well as a broad educational campaign, as general avenues toward world organization.[18]

Two other conferences were held at The Hague in 1899 and 1907, where U.S. legal experts put forth ideas in an international setting. Discussions of international law and arms limitation led to the creation of a Permanent Court of Arbitration. As a result, an unprecedented number of international disputes were resolved through the signing of treaties (over 130 from 1899 to 1910). These successful conferences at The Hague imbued the American peace movement with an air of legitimacy; membership went up accordingly.[19]

Yet as Americans became active abroad, ambiguities persisted as to the degree and method of their involvement. A strong tradition of Washingtonian isolationism persisted, stirring fears of foreign contacts and entangling treaties with other powers. The views of emerging corporations, which hailed the expansion of trade and investment as essential to the continued health and growth of the American economy, won many converts. As John Crosby Brown told the Lake Mohonk conference in 1900, "The world in all financial and commercial matters is becoming so closely knit together, so entirely one, that the slightest disturbance in any one place is immediately felt in every other part of the world. Those who have carefully watched matters of international finance believe that this condition . . . has come to stay."[20] Increased political dealings with foreign powers seemed necessary to protect American economic interests; they also proved flattering to American self-esteem and to aspirations for great-power status.

After 1900, the Lake Mohonk conferences began seeking more men like Brown, who had contacts among political leaders, international lawyers, and big business. These members, nearly all of whom were also involved in domestic progressive reforms, such as temperance, missionary efforts abroad, and social purity, began to see connections between international and domestic problems. The rapid immigration rates and the rise of industrialization in the West had led to a number of riots in the late 1800s that undoubtedly still bothered many of these turn-of-the-century peace advocates. The Haymarket riot of 1886, the Pullman strike of 1894, the William McKinley assassination of 1901 — all triggered fears of social discontent and turbulence. Reformers wanted to create order in a modern world riddled with anxiety-producing social changes. The peace movement, according to Marchand, "expressed ideas attractive to a disturbed national elite. Anxieties about social disorganization, class antagonisms, industrial violence, and declining social homogeneity engendered both a fear and distrust of lower classes and immigrant groups, and a desire . . . to restore social harmony."[21] Thus, internationalists' concerns about turbulent markets blended with their fears of unrest on American city streets to shape the progressive peace movement.

LEGITIMATION: LIFTING THE PEACE MOVEMENT UP FROM SENTIMENTALISM

By 1905, the Lake Mohonk conferences touted a guest list of truly important people: a Supreme Court justice, a Hague Court member, and the president of the philanthropic Carnegie Institution. Lawyers and businessmen shared a common bond in their dislike of other, more emotional, crusade-oriented peace societies. Frederick Lynch, of the Church Peace Union, expressed his pleasure when "leading statesmen, jurists, clergymen, college presidents and financiers of the land" became more influential than "members of the peace cult," who earlier comprised the ranks of peace advocates.[22] The kinds of men Lynch favored, he believed, could influence national policy with the authority, power, and practicality that would make peace activism "respectable," or as Marchand later wrote, to bring it "up from sentimentalism."[23]

Progressive newcomers to the peace movement imbued it with progressive values: a vigorous masculinity, reason, and practicality. Reason implies a need for order, and order was what progressives thought would bring sanity out of the spiraling numbers of immigrants whose arrival threatened the tranquility of middle- and upper-class American society. Peace advocates, ever optimistic, tended to think of men as rational creatures, who, when educated, could be relied upon to act morally. "The roots of [the pre-war peace movement] were complex," wrote the historian Michael A. Lutzker. "In the largest sense, the peace movement was perhaps the ultimate expression of the nineteenth century's faith in progress. The great technological advances gave rise to a belief that mankind was on the way to solving its age-old problems of war, disease, and poverty by the application of reason and science."[24]

Gone, then, were the emotional appeals made by older peace groups with their roots extending back into antebellum Romanticism, which progressive-minded peace workers saw as inefficient and lacking in empirical results. Officially, progressive peace organizations emphasized businesslike efficiency and reason in their programs.[25] But the irrational aspects of their work were never far from the surface.

The new peace movement resulted in a shift in leadership positions. Women, such as the former abolitionists Mary Livermore and Alice Stone Blackwell, dominated the nineteenth-century peace movement, but during the Progressive Era, men wrested the movement from its emotional beginnings in the abolitionist movement. They "elevated" the pacifist cause by making it rational, businesslike, and scientific.

Women, however, did not simply relinquish their influence.[26] Women comprised a large part of progressive reform; they were equally active in progressive pacifism. Women's place within society — a place that restricted them from holding powerful positions in all categories of public life because of their gender — affected how they constructed their identity within the progressive class.

Gender consciousness resonated in all areas of society, and the peace movement was no exception. In general, the move toward a professional peace movement — recruiting men from business, law, and science — meant a masculinized movement. Of course, many women, too, were pursuing professional careers during this period, but, for the most part, they had not yet entered the occupations that the peace movement valued. Wiebe described the feelings men held toward women who entered "acceptable" professions, such as teaching and social work, and women's compliance with those expectations: "Men did not usually feel threatened until women's activities pushed past the stereotypes. They seldom did. . . . Tacit, mutually accepted limits accounted for women's remarkably smooth arrival into a professional middle class."[27] As the progressive peace movement evolved, some women would cross the boundary line of acceptable behavior, while others helped men maintain that line. The role of women in society thus became a permanent disruption undercutting the solidity of the progressive class.

THE PROGRESSIVE PACIFIST IDEOLOGY OF INTERNATIONALISM

As men assumed dominance over women in the progressive peace movement, progressive pacifists also assumed the United States would dominate international relations. The United States emerged as a world leader during the Progressive Era, and as the historian David S. Patterson wrote, "[reformers] accepted America's rise to world power as largely inevitable and essentially beneficient, and they viewed the peace movement as the most useful vehicle for convincing American governmental leaders to promote a harmonious international order."[28] On the issues of international arbitration, and other peace-keeping machinery, progressive pacifists intended no curtailment of American sovereignty or of American nationalism. According to Marchand, "Most spokesmen for the peace movement assumed that the process of building world peace would not mean the surrender of any powers or principles or policies of the United States, but rather the gradual extension of American influence through the acceptance abroad of American principles, habits of thought, and institutions."[29] Hamilton Holt, editor of the progressive journal *Independent*, reflected these sentiments when he referred to the harmonious relationship among the American states as a model for the future of the world's nations: "It seems destined that America lead in this [peace] movement. The United States is the world in miniature."[30]

THE WORLD PEACE FOUNDATION

The World Peace Foundation, the peace group Hamilton Holt belonged to, represented pre-war progressive peace organizations devoted to the idea of international cooperation and organization and to educating the public about the use of rational, nonviolent means to end international conflicts. The WPF also exemplified the coalition-building method used by progressive reformers to harness the energies of diverse interests in the name of a single cause. In its early years, the foundation did not conceive of a particular plan to end war but instead sought to organize the American peace movement to achieve greater efficiency and effectiveness. The foundation's philosophy and attitudes toward war and international relations reflected the elitism of the progressive men who formed the core of the antiwar movement in the early twentieth century. The WPF, then, served as a barometer of how the progressive ideology of efficiency and reason, and the strategy of coalition building, played out in the years preceding the First World War.[31]

Edwin Ginn, proprietor of the Boston publishing firm of Ginn and Company, philanthropist, participant in the Lake Mohonk conferences, and founder of the World Peace Foundation, perceived a lack of accessible literature in the peace movement. "We spend," he asked rhetorically, "hundreds of millions a year for war; can we afford to spend one million for peace?"[32]

Ginn believed that funding peace rather than war would make for a more peaceful world. But his ideas went deeper than simply throwing money at the problem. As he surveyed the sixty-three peace societies then in existence, he perceived a lack of leadership among them.[33] He quickly called for the worldwide cooperation of industrialists and capitalists to help solve the problem of international violence. If businessmen were to provide leadership, Ginn was convinced that the masses could be educated to follow them. The purpose of the WPF, then, was to instill the proper ideology in the public by educating common citizens about how to settle disputes between nations through the use of reason instead of force. To that end, the WPF's early goal was to place a series of informative pamphlets, at minimal cost, in the hands of existing peace organizations, librarians, school teachers, newspapermen, and clergy. These molders of public opinion would inculcate the public with a from-the-top-down flow of information.

Ginn also detected alarming overlap in the work accomplished by existing peace societies. He imagined that integrating existing groups under an umbrella organization could make the peace movement work more efficiently. He also wanted the WPF to represent a coalition of farmers, laborers, and women's groups. These diverse organizations were part of Ginn's overall scheme to disseminate his ideology among other, progressive-minded people.

In addition to peace advocacy, the WPF's goal was to promote acceptance of the dominant social order in American society, through its method of coalition building, and internationally, through the institution of a federation of nations, international law (based on American democracy), and a world court. Although the WPF's records showed an eagerness to merge with granges, labor, and women, in reality its energies (and most of its money) went toward building alliances with people much more reflective of its own leadership: the expert lawyers and businessmen being wooed by the peace movement's leaders. The peace advocates' primary concern was to shift emphasis away from emotional appeal to rational, practical-minded men who would infuse the organizations with respectability.

The upper echelons of the World Peace Foundation revealed its preference for men and women of power. Its board of ten trustees included five academic deans and presidents, two businessmen, one U.S. Representative, a Unitarian minister, and a lawyer. The board of seven directors consisted of three academics, three journalists, and one lawyer. Among the WPF's Advisory Council members were Jane Addams, Lucia Ames Mead, and Booker T. Washington. Most of the leaders of the WPF served together in other peace societies, such as the New York and Massachusetts Peace Societies, and in other reform activity, so they had similar interests.[34]

The foundation's most active directors between 1910 and 1914 were David Starr Jordan and Edwin Mead. These men, along with Ginn, formulated the ideas the WPF supported. Mead also prepared excerpts from WPF pamphlets, with titles such as "War Not Inevitable," "The Grange and Peace," and "Club Women and the Peace Movement," to be printed in newspapers. "One can often bring down game with three hundred words," he postulated, "where three thousand bullets would not pierce the skin."[35] By the time war broke out in 1914, the foundation had circulated 300,000 copies of several pamphlets written by WPF members, including articles reproduced from other sources. WPF publications were the mainstay of the organization's educational efforts.

Despite the smooth operations of its publishing activities, however, Ginn still worried about a lack of efficiency within the foundation. He argued that hiring a business manager to coordinate the WPF's activities would produce optimum effectiveness. To guard against overlap, he dispersed its operations into a number of organizational branches, including a Special Department for Women, a Finance Committee, a Publicity and Propaganda Bureau, and a Committee of Organizations, Colleges, Universities, and Schools.

The WPF also circulated its ideas through the efforts of its public speakers. It sponsored the speaking tours of Norman Angell (British author of *The Great Illusion*, the most widely read antiwar book at the time)[36] and the Austrian peace activist Baroness Bertha von Suttner. In 1912 the foundation persuaded the International Chambers of Commerce to hold its meeting in Boston. Here, the chambers approved a declaration in favor of substituting judicial for armed solutions to international conflicts. Ginn scored a personal victory when Andrew Carnegie announced the creation of the Carnegie Endowment for International Peace, in response to Ginn's call for millionaires to contribute to the antiwar movement. In its first two years, then, the WPF utilized primarily the talents of an educated, wealthy elite to disseminate its views on peace. But the WPF made little use of the organizations it intended to enlist: granges, labor, and women's groups. The foundation's elitism and paternalism caused this oversight. However, the overconfident elitism they communicated to one another betrayed not rationality but *irrational* expectations of what they, as men of power and influence, could accomplish.

THE IRRATIONAL GOALS OF THE WORLD PEACE FOUNDATION

WPF leaders hoped to change the world. Using gendered language, Ginn, for example, peppered his letters with sentences such as, "We shall be much more successful in educating the people by *impregnating the whole journalistic profession* with our ideas." "We have got a big job on our hands. . . . [it is] to *re-educate the world.*" "He [Samuel McDonald] is a good man. He might be a very efficient man in organizing the *press of the world* [emphasis added]."[37] Such sweeping generalities could hardly be called "rational."

Although Ginn wanted to build coalitions among various interests, he spoke primarily of "the masses," rather than particular people belonging to specific groups. He betrayed the progressives' and upper class's fears of "antagonizing the masses" and its paternalistic attitude that "the people of the world are yet creeping. They can't stand alone and they can't comprehend such things." Edwin Mead, too, lumped immigrants from all nations into his single plan of Americanizing them, "because then they send this [American civilization] back to Europe."[38] This attitude coincided with the ludicrously sweeping changes the WPF hoped to make: If the masses were all ignorant, then it was necessary simply to educate all of them, en masse. In the WPF's irrational overconfidence, in its adherence to the progressive notion of "civility," and in its paternalistic attitude toward the very people with whom it hoped to merge, it undermined its coalition-building efforts.

WOMEN IN THE WORLD PEACE FOUNDATION

Although the World Peace Foundation differed from other pre-war peace societies by recruiting women, it ultimately dropped its female speaker and its Women's Department. The foundation took note of the multitude of women's organizations in the United States, as it did of the farmers' granges and organized labor, and decided to enlist these groups in the cause of peace. The idea was to establish a Women's Department that would carry out the foundation's general goal of educating the public.

However, the WPF's dealings with women were far from supportive. The relationship between the Women's Department director, Anna Sturgis Duryea, and the rest of the foundation's directors and its founder, Edwin Ginn, was never a happy one. Duryea's function within the WPF was to lecture to women's clubs and other organizations, such as patriotic societies, college associations, and public schools. Her presentations promoted the WPF's philosophy and goals but without a particular woman's perspective. For her services, she received a salary of $1,500 in 1911. In 1914, she asked for and was granted an increase in salary to $2,400. However, in her last year as WPF speaker, her salary was reduced to $2,000.

The World Peace Foundation used progressive barometers, such as the notion of efficiency, to measure Duryea's performance. In a 1910 report about her activities, Mead reflected the male leadership's uncertain, cautious attitude toward her: "Her work has steadily grown in popularity and *efficiency*; and it would be well if there could be half a dozen women doing this kind of work . . . although whether it should be done permanently under our auspices or ultimately under the direction of the reorganized American Peace Society, is a matter for future consideration."[39]

Apparently, although the WPF liked Duryea's work, its leaders were not anxious to include her within their program. The promotional literature on Duryea's speeches indicated that their content did not differ from the topics discussed elsewhere in WPF pamphlets, so the men's attitude did not stem from ideological differences.

At a December 18, 1911, meeting of the Finance Committee, her request for a salary increase was granted, albeit grudgingly and with this curious provision:

In the Finance Committee's judgment there is some doubt as to whether the World Peace Foundation is justified in incurring so large an expenditure for the kind of work Mrs. Duryea is doing, even recognizing to the fullest extent the efficiency with which she is performing that work, therefore the acting chief director should notify her that if she should have an opportunity to better her financial status during the year, on reasonable notice, this committee would recommend that she be permitted to avail herself of such opportunity, particularly in view of the feeling of this committee of doubt as to whether this sort of work should be continued after the ensuing year.[40]

In 1913 Duryea found a way to make her services harmonize more closely with WPF standards. Whereas she had formerly lectured for free, she was now charging a fee. Ginn took pleasure in noting that, now, "people are willing to pay for your lectures. That is the best evidence of their value," he reasoned.[41]

But by the next year, the foundation was in the process of fazing out both Duryea and its Women's Department. At a Board of Trustees meeting in 1914, members announced that Duryea had been absorbed into another branch of the WPF, reflecting her loss of status: her position was to assist the chief director of the Department of Publicity and Propaganda and work "under his general direction." In October 1915, the directors of the WPF voted to discontinue the Women's Department altogether. In 1916 the Finance Committee's report included these words regarding Duryea: "The finance committee understands that she [Duryea] has rendered no services . . . and believes we are not warranted in making future payments to her, certainly no payments in the nature of a pension or retirement fund are warranted, either as a matter of law, or as a matter of sound administration." On June 5, 1916, the Board of Trustees voted to pay Duryea $1,000 "provided she will sign a written statement releasing the WPF from all further claims."[42] Duryea had apparently requested compensation she felt she deserved, whereas the WPF disagreed. In any case, the foundation did not feel that Duryea or the Woman's Department was worthy of further funding.

In at least two other instances, Ginn and Mead expressed displeasure with women colleagues, with one exception. The WPF sponsored a speaking tour by an Austrian aristocrat, the Baroness von Suttner. Ginn gushed over his idea of "making [the baroness's lecture program] a hundred times more efficient as the old method of free lectures." In this case, as with Duryea, "efficient" meant charging a fee. "Every one of those [women's] clubs," wrote Ginn, "should be required to pay a good fee to hear the woman that has done more than any other to bring about desired reforms."[43] Taken together, the WPF's experiences with Duryea and Suttner showed an organization so preoccupied with efficiency that it ignored the content of either Duryea's or the baroness's speeches. The WPF's leaders were uncertain as to what role, if any, women ought to play in their organization. The foundation did not favor suffrage and therefore did not perceive of women as political participants in society.

The WPF's perceptions of women were revealed in how it understood men and masculinity. Ginn, for example, discussed the possibilities of recruiting a new man to join the foundation: "We don't want any half men if we can help it. We want whole men or none. Undivided attention to our work is my motto in the future." The bulk of Ginn's correspondence with other foundation members revealed his preoccupation with and insistence upon ambition, drive, and hard work — work free of "emotional excitement."[44] In short, Ginn believed that "the right kind of men" should "man" the peace movement, using a combination of a Protestant work ethic, individualism, and businesslike efficiency, which left little room for feminine influence in the WPF. A further elimination of a female WPF member was yet to come.

THE FIRST FEMINIST PEACE ORGANIZATION: THE WOMAN'S PEACE PARTY

The problems that some female peace workers such as Duryea faced within established peace societies led them to finally form a separate pacifist organization based on the "so-called feminine values" to which the women at the Lake Mohonk conferences had alluded. But the pacifist organization they created, in its national form, did little to challenge acceptable gender roles within society.

The outbreak of war in 1914 catalyzed the women into forming the Woman's Peace Party. On August 29, 1914, more than 1,500 women, dressed in white gowns and beating muffled drums, marched down New York's streets in silent protest against the war. The Parade Committee that organized this demonstration included women's-rights activists from a variety of reform causes, ranging from suffrage (Carrie Chapman Catt) to social work (Lillian Wald and Lavinia Dock) and labor (Mary Deier and Rose Schneiderman). Committee leader Fanny Garrison Villard, daughter of the abolitionist William Lloyd Garrison, intended to organize the marchers into a permanent, all-female peace society, one that would function as a "new moral movement" within the established peace movement.

Villard expressed disappointment in the male organizations' lack of active response to the outbreak of war.[45]

From a feminist standpoint, the marchers reasoned that women suffer the most during a war, both as civilian victims and as caretakers of other casualties of war, whom wives, mothers, female nurses, and social workers help heal. The committee favored new tactical ideas, such as public marches, which differed from the approach to peace work taken by the male-dominated societies. The Parade Committee expressed horror over the conflict overseas and requested that President Wilson act as a mediator to bring a swift conclusion to the war.

By November 1914, the women were receiving news from the international suffrage network that there was no end in sight to the battles. The reports they received were filled with accounts of brutality and suffering. Two European suffragists, Rosika Schwimmer and Emmeline Pethick-Lawrence, came to the United States on speaking tours, reinforcing the news reports that women had been hearing. Along with Schwimmer and Pethick-Lawrence, two New York suffragists, Madeline Z. Doty and Crystal Eastman, arranged the first formal feminist peace organization in U.S. history, which culminated in the Woman's Peace Party. Heady as the organizational meetings must have been, these young but politically savvy women realized that if they were to influence male politicians, they needed to enlist the help of women already accepted in progressive circles. They turned to Catt and Addams, both respected activists in their fifties.[46]

Addams hesitated to form an all-female group, contending that it contradicted the goal of sexual equality. Catt did not want to commit suffragists to working for peace, fearing disruption within the women's rights movement. But ultimately, both women relented. Catt complained to Addams that the established peace societies, "all well-endowed," were "very masculine in their point of view." Furthermore, "It would seem that they have as little use of women and their points of view as have the militarists."[47] Addams concurred: "I quite agree with you as to the masculine management of the existing Peace Societies." She explained further:

The women of this country were lulled into inattention to the great military question of the war by reading the many books put forth by great pacifists who had studied the question deeply and who announced that there could never be another world war. But when it was found that their conclusions were false and the great war came, the women of this country waited for the pacifists to move, and when they heard nothing from them — and they have heard nothing from the men of this country — they decided all too late to get together themselves.[48]

Anna Garlin Spencer, too, agreed that the established peace societies did not provide women an opportunity to express their attitudes toward war.

As it evolved, the WPP kept the coalition-building strategy of the older societies but granted more autonomy to its state and local branches. The party represented a coalition of interests from temperance (Women's Christian Temperance Union) to labor (Women's Trade Union League), and included World Peace Foundation members Duryea and Fannie Fern Andrews.[49]

SEPARATE BUT EQUAL: THE WPP
AND WOMAN SUFFRAGE

The WPP platform suggested a group committed to extending political power to those outside the margins of government but not solely by educating the masses. The platform called for the enlisting of "all American women in arousing the nations to respect the sacredness of human life and to abolish war." The party advocated organized opposition to military education, the education of youth for peace, democratic control of foreign policy, and the "further humaniz[ing of] governments by the extension of the franchise to women." "Equally with men pacifists," the document read, "we understand that planned for, legalized wholesale human slaughter is today the sum of all villainies, . . . as human beings and the mother-half of humanity, we demand that our right be consulted in the settlement of questions . . . [that we have] a share in deciding between war and peace in all the courts of high debate: within the home, the school, the church, the industrial order, and the state."[50] Proud homemakers, the WPP envisioned women within a traditional "private" female sphere: in the home as mothers, and as a moral force within the family. The WPP preamble trumpeted the position of the woman's sphere as equal to the state, and insisted that women gain access to the male — the "public" — sphere.

The WPP's initial unity under a feminist banner, however, quickly broke down. During the WPP conventions the members exhibited disagreement surrounding the proper role of women outside the home. At the first annual meeting in January 1916, one of the first items of contention was the question of suffrage, and, by extension, of a woman's place in politics. As drafted by the WPP National Executive Board, the constitution of the WPP declared the party to be the U.S. branch of the International Committee of Women for Permanent Peace (ICW). This body had two planks: The first, suffrage; the second, peace. Some of the women assembled, particularly those from Massachusetts, had difficulty accepting the alliance of the WPP with the international body because of the perceived priority of the suffrage plank.

Lucia Ames Mead, secretary of the WPP and representative from Massachusetts, told the gathering that she could not accommodate antisuffragists in Massachusetts once the WPP affiliated with the ICW. In response, Addams, chair of the WPP, admitted that the ICW placed more emphasis on suffrage than did the platform of the WPP — the WPP had merely included suffrage as one of eleven planks and asked only that members be in "substantial agreement" with its platform. The international group, by contrast, had made suffrage a sine qua non of belonging to that body.

Addams tried to illuminate the importance of suffrage within the female peace movement. She explained that the idea of The Hague conference had had its inception among members of the international suffrage movement. The congress was started by suffragists who believed that a peace meeting could and should be held in time of war. "It is" said Addams, "only the women who have been accustomed to suffrage and other unpopular causes *who will come out for peace in a country at war*" [emphasis added]. She suggested that the assembly rethink the WPP's alliance with the ICW noting that the ICW's emphasis on suffrage could not be changed. Subsequently, she challenged the assembly: "Are the two things [suffrage and peace] compatible?" Finally, the group voted to maintain the WPP as a section of the ICW without really agreeing on an answer to the question.[51]

During this debate, Villard provided the voice of a dedicated pacifist and of a feminist who conceived of women as moral leaders. She spoke in ways that clearly went beyond acceptable boundaries. "I personally considered it a great weakness on our part that we invited to our membership those people who were in 'substantial agreement' with us," she said. "I would have liked it better if we could have said: 'All those who are fully in sympathy with us, shall join us!' . . . leaving no loophole [for those whose opinions differ]."[52] She repeated this absolutist position throughout the debate.

The women's anxieties over the suffrage issue reflected their uncertainty about women's proper role in politics. The WPP preamble and platform showed a group of women anxious to participate in government. For example, the preamble stated that women demanded their right to be "consulted in the settlement of questions concerning not alone the life of individuals, but of nations to be recognized and respected." But the debate during the 1916 convention revealed that some women within the WPP were leery of suffrage and of assuming such powers.

Notable issues discussed at the convention reflected the women's anxieties about immigration and Americanization, worries common to other progressives. And, like other reformers, the women relied on "experts" to help them solve problems. One resolution passed by the group favored a bill to allow the federal government to have control of all unnaturalized residents in the United States. Specifically, the WPP discussed the case of an Italian alien who had been lynched in New Orleans, and when Louisiana refused to prosecute the man accused of the murder, the federal government's hands were tied. "This," claimed Mead, "is in the interest of justice." Sophonisba Breckenridge made a spurious connection between this measure and peace. She reasoned that the measure was needed in order to "remove the possible sources of friction between nations." The resolution passed immediately, with no dissent.

But Anita Newcomb McGee thought the problem required more explanation. Some of the WPP members, in a previous informal gathering, had accused California suffragists of "cutting off" the access of Japanese and Chinese women to the WPP; McGee denied this, saying that "we only cut them off . . . until sufficient time as they have been able to assimilate with us." McGee claimed to respect unassimilated groups but confessed that their "alien culture" proved too great a stumbling block. She then suggested that the WPP add a call for a committee of "experts" to debate the resolution; significantly, these experts were supposed to be "men who are thoroughly competent"[53] to determine how the government ought to deal with alien immigrants. The women agreed to rely on "experts" to solve the problem for them — male experts, at that. Even the skeptical Villard did not question the facile link between Americanizing aliens (the real impetus behind the resolution) and working for peace.

Finally, the members voted on whether women ought to be included at the proposed third Hague conference on world peace. The existing amendment to the WPP constitution insisted that conference delegates represent social, financial, labor, and scientific interests. The group approved the amendment without including women in the list, but Addams decided to prod the group into making an addition.

In response to Addams's proposal, Mead declared, "I should vote against any such action at The Hague. At present we have never had a woman who is a judge, diplomat, captain of industry, or a woman who has had international experience so as to make her a great authority on international law . . . it would be a premature action." Mead apparently agreed with Edwin Ginn, and other progressives, who believed the peace movement should be "manned" by male professionals. Mary Cruttenden Percy nodded her assent. "I understand that the foreigners are not, as yet, as advanced in their ideas about women." (Apparently, Percy had already forgotten Schwimmer and Pethick-Lawrence, the European women partly responsible for the formation of the WPP.) On the other side, another member suggested that "a body of women should be the last ones to be afraid of having a woman on an international body. . . . And as for being judges or diplomats, it seems to me the conferences of the past have failed because we have had too many diplomats and judges." Villard, speaking as an essentialist feminist, agreed: "I want to suggest that women might be experts on the higher law, the moral law."[54] This time the feminists carried the day, and the WPP proposed that women be included at the third Hague conference.

A PARTY OF PROTEST?

After the war began in Europe, some women were either released from their duties within the male-dominated peace groups or they were not granted leadership or powerful positions within those groups, so they left of their own accord (although many women, including Addams, Eastman, and Mead, continued their memberships and activism in mixed-gender groups). However, the debates that occurred at the WPP convention showed that women, such as Duryea, Rose Dabney Forbes, Addams, and Mead, all of whom worked in older peace societies, retained some of the progressive characteristics that imbued groups such as the WPF. The dichotomy of direct democracy versus elite rule, one of those characteristics, was also problematic for WPP members. Their preamble, platform, and constitution, which demanded that women be given an equal voice in the pacifist movement, provided a false front for some women in the group who were, in truth, less willing to share political power with men. The only positive step taken toward granting women access to male-dominated institutions was in the recommendation that women be included at the Hague conference, a move that would not have occurred without the patient goading of Jane Addams. The WPP, more often than not, handed over questions to unnamed "experts" or wanted to drop entirely matters that they felt unable to deal with. "I would very much like to remove the word 'protest' everywhere it is used in these recommendations," said Mrs. Gilson Gardner, in a statement very reflective of the WPP convention. "I think it is a great mistake for us to appear as a party of protest."[55] In truth, as a national body, the WPP did not wish to disrupt the traditional sphere of womanhood. Eventually, some of the more radical women with the WPP would challenge women's customary role within society, but that move awaited further developments.

The WPP's spokeswoman for the "moral, higher law," Villard, voiced several suggestions also in keeping with a more essentialist stance. But for the most part, her opinions were voted down. Villard had maintained that women reacted to the war differently from men. Whereas the WPF deemed uncontrolled emotion one of the *causes* of war, the WPP members stated that their emotional reaction to the war was a basis for their activism *against* war. But, in many cases, the WPP's adherence to the progressive ideology of elite expertise prevented them from carrying their moral imperative further than they did.

NOTES

1. John A. Thompson, *Reformers and War: American Progressive Publicists and the First World War* (Cambridge: Cambridge University Press, 1987), 5–6.

2. Nancy S. Dye, "Introduction," in *Gender, Class, Race and Reform in the Progressive Era*, ed. Nancy S. Dye and Noralee Frankel (Lexington: University of Kentucky Press, 1991), 9.

3. David Kennedy, "Overview: The Progressive Era," *Historian* 36 (May 1975): 454; Richard Hofstadter, *The Age of Reform, from Bryan to F.D.R.* (New York: Vintage, 1955).

4. Gabriel Kolko, *The Triumph of Conservatism: A Reinterpretation of American History* (New York: Free Press, 1968), 305, 286–287; James Weinstein, *The Corporate Ideal in the Liberal State, 1900–1918* (Boston: Beacon Press, 1968), 5–6; Kennedy, "Overview," 454.

5. Robert H. Wiebe, *The Search for Order: 1877–1920* (New York: Hill and Wang, 1967).

6. John D. Buenker, "Essay," in *Progressivism*, ed. John D. Buenker, John C. Burnham, and Robert M. Crunden (Cambridge, Mass.: Schenkman, 1977), 31.

7. James Parker Martin, "The American Peace Movement and the Progressive Era, 1910–1917" (Ph.D. diss., Rice University, 1975), 11–16.

8. Nancy S. Dye and Noralee Frankel, eds., *Gender, Class, Race and Reform in the Progressive Era* (Lexington: University of Kentucky Press, 1991), 3.

9. Anthony Giddens, *The Class Structure of Advanced Societies*, 2nd ed. (London: Hutchinson, 1981), 132, 177–197 as cited by Carroll Smith-Rosenberg, "Writing History: Language, Class and Gender" in *Feminist Studies — Critical Studies*, ed. Teresa D'Lauretis (Bloomington: Indiana University Press, 1986), 34. I have based my ideas about the meaning of class from this Smith-Rosenberg essay.

10. Wiebe, *Search for Order*, 120–121.

11. Antonio Gramsci, *Selections from the Prison Notebooks*, ed. Quintin

Hoare and Geoffrey Nowell Smith (New York: International Publishers, 1971), 326.

12.   Gail Bederman, *Manliness and Civilization: A Cultural History of Gender and Race in the United States, 1880–1917* (Chicago: University of Chicago, 1995), 6–7; David Starr Jordan, "An Indictment, by David Starr Jordan, Chancellor of Stanford University," SR 12.2, WPP Papers, SCPC; Paul U. Kellogg, "Statement to the President," 28 February 1917, reel 10.1, American Union Against Militarism (hereafter abbreviated AUAM) Papers, SCPC.

13.   Samuel Haber, *Efficiency and Uplift: Scientific Management in the Progressive Era, 1890–1920* (Chicago: University of Chicago Press, 1964), ix–xii.

14.   Martin, "American Peace Movement," p. 91n.

15.   Carroll Smith-Rosenberg, "Writing History: Language, Class and Gender," in *Feminist Studies — Critical Studies*, ed. Teresa D'Lauretis (Bloomington: Indiana University Press, 1986), 34.

16.   C. Roland Marchand, *The American Peace Movement and Social Reform, 1898–1918* (Princeton, N.J.: Princeton University Press, 1972), 19.

17.   Charles R. Howlett, "Women Pacifists in America: Women's Views at the Lake Mohonk Conferences for International Arbitration, 1895–1916," *Peace Research* 21 (January 1989): 28.

18.   David S. Patterson, "An Interpretation of the American Peace Movement, 1898–1914," in *Peace Movements in America*, ed. Charles Chatfield (New York: Schocken Books, 1973), 22.

19.   Peter Filene, "The World Peace Foundation and Progressivism: 1910–1918," *New England Quarterly* 36 (December 1963): 484–501.

20.   Brown quoted in "The Pacifist as Militarist: A Critique of the American Peace Movement, 1898–1914," by Michael A. Lutzker, *Societas* 5 (Spring 1975): 91.

21.   Marchand, *Peace Movement and Social Reform*, 36.

22.   Lynch quoted in ibid., 21.

23.   Marchand titled his first chapter about the innovations in pre-war peace organizations in *Peace Movement and Social Reform* "Up From Sentimentalism."

24.   Michael A. Lutzker, "The Pacifist as Militarist: A Critique of the American Peace Movement, 1898–1914," *Societas* 5 (Spring 1975): 89.

25.   Marchand, *Peace Movement and Social Reform*, 21–22; see also Patterson, "Interpretation," 29, for a discussion of pacifists' views of the need to control men's emotions.

26.   Harriet Hyman Alonso, *Peace as a Woman's Issue: A History of the U.S. Movement for World Peace and Women's Rights* (Syracuse, N.Y.: Syracuse University Press, 1993), chap. 2, "Developing a Feminist-Pacifist Consciousness, 1820–1914," where she mentions women's leadership positions within established peace societies and women's organizations interested in peace, such as the Women's Christian Temperance Union, which linked militarism with the abuse of alcohol.

27. Wiebe, *Search for Order*, 122.

28. Patterson, "Interpretation," 23.

29. Marchand, *Peace Movement and Social Reform*, 35–36.

30. Quoted in Patterson, "Interpretation," 20.

31. Filene, "World Peace Foundation," 478.

32. Quoted in ibid., 480.

33. Filene counted sixty-three societies existing in 1914, p. 479 fn. 1.

34. "History of the World Peace Foundation," 1963, World Peace Foundation (hereafter abbreviated WPF) Papers, SCPC; Filene, "World Peace Foundation," 481–482.

35. Quoted in Filene, "World Peace Foundation," 484.

36. Norman Angell, *The Great Illusion, A Study of the Relation of Military Power in Nations to Their Economic and Social Advantage*, 1911 (reprint, ed. S. J. Stears, New York: Garland Press, 1972). The book criticized theories of Social Darwinism, which Angell believed led to war.

37. Ginn to Mead and Holt, 16 May 1912; Ginn to Dutton, 23 May 1912; Ginn to Mead and Jordan, 29 March 1912, DG 55, Box 5, WPF Papers, SCPC.

38. Ginn to Dutton, 5 May 1912; Ginn to Henrik C. Andersen, 10 July 1913; Mead to Nicholas Murray Butler, 9 July 1913, DG 55, Box 5, WPF Papers, SCPC.

39. Board of Directors Report; Minutes, 1910–1915, DG 55, Box 2, WPF Papers, SCPC.

40. Finance Committee Minutes, 1910–1915, DG 55, Box 2, WPF Papers, SCPC.

41. Ginn to Duryea, 20 August 1913, DG 55, Box 4, WPF Papers, SCPC.

42. Samuel T. Dutton, "1914 Report of the Committee on Organizations to the Trustees of the WPF"; "Minutes of the Board of Trustees, 1915–1925," DG 55, Box 2, WPF Papers, SCPC.

43. Ginn to Hofer, 25 May 1912, DG 55, Box 2, WPF Papers, SCPC. Fannie Fern Andrews and Mary Hofer were among other women of whom Ginn and Mead spoke disapprovingly. Ginn's primary complaint was that WPF people were not performing efficiently. Other WPF leaders were similarly obsessed with efficiency. The word appears repeatedly in WPF reports, committee meeting minutes, and correspondence. David Starr Jordan's contract, for example, reads "could be terminated if he is not sufficiently efficient," DG 55, Box 2, Minutes 1910–1915, WPF Papers, SCPC.

44. Ginn to Mead, 23 July 1912; Ginn to John Mott, 13 Feb. 1912, DG 55, Box 2, WPF Papers, SCPC.

45. Villard quoted in Alonso, *Peace as a Women's Issue*, 57.

46. Ibid., 58–59.

47. Ibid., 62; Catt to Addams, 16 December 1914, SR 12.1, WPP Papers, SCPC.

48. Addams to Catt, 21 December 1914, SR 12.1, WPP Papers, SCPC; Addams to Catt, 10 January 1915, SR 12.1, WPP Papers, SCPC.

49.   Barbara J. Steinson, *American Women's Activism in World War I* (New York: Garland Press, 1982), 40–41; Marie Louise Degen, *A History of the Woman's Peace Party*, 1939 (reprint, New York: Garland Press, 1972), 39.

50.   "Preamble and Platform" 10 January 1915; amended 11 January 1916, SR 12.1, WPP Papers, SCPC. The platform was authored by Anna Garlin Spencer; the phrase "mother-half of humanity" was borrowed from Emmeline Pethick-Lawrence.

51.   The question is not a simple one. Berenice Carroll, et al.'s *The Role of Women in Conflict and Peace: Papers* (Ann Arbor: University of Michigan Center for Continuing Education of Women, 1977) includes an essay on the theoretical links between feminism and pacifism. "Annual Meeting January 1916" minutes, sessions 1–5, SR 12.1, WPP Papers, SCPC.

52.   "Annual Meeting January 1916."

53.   Ibid.

54.   Ibid.

55.   Ibid.

3

The Progressive Peace Movement's March Toward Military Preparedness

The progressive peace movement's hope that in the twentieth century conflict between nations would be solved by reason rather than violence disintegrated when war broke out in Europe in June 1914. Embedded in the progressives' preference for "civilization" over "barbarity" were assumptions about enlightened "reason" over instinctual "violence." Notwithstanding their horror over the bloodshed in Europe, these assumptions ultimately helped trap progressive pacifists into responding militarily to armed conflict. For if all the savage "Hun" understood was violence, then he must be met with armed resistance.

But the progressives' conception of "civilization" often contradicted itself. Some progressives believed that too much "civilization," by which they meant an overabundance of leisure time and the excessive consumption of material goods, had resulted in a lazy, flaccid, and dispirited people. The progressive journalist Edward Devine insisted that the nation needed *something* to bring the renewed "life, vigor, efficiency, power of creation, and capacity for enjoyment" that were otherwise missing in American society. Devine and others would ultimately approve of increased military appropriations to lift American spirits, *if* they were accompanied by welfare measures that progressives advocated.[1]

Other middle-class men and women utilized the discourse of civilization to reinforce the power and authority of white manhood. For example, on the one hand, some progressives, such as former U.S. President

Theodore Roosevelt, called for increased militarism to reinvigorate what they saw as an "overcivilized" society; they concomitantly provoked fears of a defenseless white race. On the other hand, progressive pacifists such as David Starr Jordan warned that a proliferation of arms would lead to war, which would bring "subsequent impoverishment, physical and mental, to the [white] race." Progressives' ideas about civilization, which were imbued with notions of racial supremacy and male power, played into their ultimate acceptance of increased military expenditures.[2]

PROGRESSIVE ADVOCATES OF MILITARY PREPAREDNESS

Shortly after shots were fired in Europe, arms advocates within the progressive movement began a campaign designed to ready the United States for war. Military activists successfully formulated their drive in terms of an active, masculine patriotism and democracy, which coincided with progressives' desire to reform the nation into a stronger democracy. As a result, many progressive pacifists were drawn into their fold.

Initially, most progressive reformers were solidly opposed to an arms build-up. During the first few months of the European war, according to the historian Arthur Link, neutrality pervaded American sentiment. Politicians and the American public perceived European and American interests as completely separate. But the submarine crisis of 1915 led to the discovery of German intrigues against American peace and neutrality and ultimately focused attention on the state of America's national defense. Link blamed German aggression for bringing the inadequate state of America's military forces before the public. Nevertheless, progressives were opposed to a build-up of armed forces. Although a small group of interventionists tried to "fire up the war spirit" among an indifferent government and public, the interventionists, wrote Link, "remained only a fractional minority before March, 1917."[3]

James P. Martin offered a different analysis in his 1975 work, "The American Peace Movement and the Progressive Era." Martin contended that the call for modernizing American forces was already a progressive issue *before* the European war began. Shocked by the inefficiency of the army and navy, reformers within the government and military appealed for change. However, agreeing with Link, Martin also described a blasé attitude in Congress and in the nation at large. The public, according to this view, needed to be informed of the dangers of military weakness. "It had become apparent to the would-be reformers," wrote Martin, "that the idea of a modern army would have to be sold to the American people."[4]

The search for civilians to campaign for increased arms—journalists, industrialists, and other politicians—was already underway before 1914. Indeed, Martin claimed, the European war created a favorable climate for militarism in the United States. Europeans and Americans alike expected the war to end quickly; when it did not, politicians and citizen groups became concerned about the United States' ability to protect and defend itself.[5]

In 1987 the historian John Thompson offered a deeper analysis of the relationship between progressives and the issue of military strength. Underlying progressives' discussion of foreign policy in this period was the potential military power of the United States, not the machinations of the Kaiser. The United States produced more steel in 1913 than Germany, Russia, and Great Britain combined, wrote Thompson, making it the only neutral nation capable of breaking the military deadlock between the warring nations. But progressive publicists rarely raised the possibility of intervention explicitly before the United States declared war.[6] Evidence for Thompson's contention appeared, for example, in a series of articles in November and December 1914 that Roosevelt published in *Outlook* magazine. Rather than mentioning the conflict raging in Europe, Roosevelt made connections between American democracy and the military obligations of its young men:

It is because the *Outlook* believes that righteous liberty in this world demands more than the mere lip service of our great democracy, that righteous liberty in the end can be obtained only through the spread of the democratic ideal for which this Nation stands, and that the spread of this ideal depends not only upon the desire and the will but also upon the power of our people, that we have long advocated the adequate military preparation of our American democracy.[7]

The question upon which progressives such as Roosevelt focused was whether America should build up its armed forces, or, in the vernacular of the day, its "preparedness." Unlike Link, Thompson did not see the progressives lined up in opposition to preparedness. Instead, he described how progressive pacifists gradually came into the preparedness camp, both through their own desire to control it and through the ability of the preparedness advocates to make it into a progressive issue. Both Martin and Thompson viewed preparedness as a political issue that emerged as a part of progressivism, whereas Link believed military enthusiasts came from outside the movement.[8]

Progressives not only battled for control of American politics, but they fought among themselves for power over their own class. Linguistically, the diverse forces within the progressive class jousted for primacy by using gendered discourse. In addition, a difference in positioning along "elitist" versus "democratic" lines determined the degree to which they accepted preparedness. Some members of the World Peace Foundation (WPF), and of the Woman's Peace Party (WPP), tended to fall into the "elitist" category. They were more likely to accept preparedness. But a new group, the American Union Against Militarism (AUAM), never completely accepted the campaign of the preparedness advocates; its members based their antipreparedness sentiment on their identity as democratic reformers and on increasingly narrow class interests. Both positions — pro- and antipreparedness — were a part of progressive discourse.

In early 1915 military activists within progressivism began a crusade to win the public's active consent for their policies. In their preparedness campaign, progressives defined themselves not only in economic terms and social terms (i.e., as the middle or professional class) but also in terms of a common intellectual and moral awareness, a common culture — "a coherent class formation," as the political theorist Walter Adamson later wrote, "united behind a single economic, political, and cultural conception of the world."[9] In the case of progressive pacifists, this worldview was known as the "international mind" — a term appearing often in the WPF, AUAM, and WPP publications and records. The term signified the spread of the democratic ideal and the exportation of the American system abroad. As Roosevelt and other preparedness supporters remarked, American hegemony in world affairs required a strong military to protect, enhance, and fortify American democratic institutions.

THE PRESS AND MILITARY PREPAREDNESS

In building consensus for their worldview, the preparedness advocates' first goal was to make Americans aware of the military impotence of their country. For example, Roosevelt accused the Wilson administration of not performing the "first duty" of a democracy, which was "to protect the persons and property of its citizens" with its military forces. In the face of such neglect, Roosevelt argued that it was up to journalists to *invent* opinion sympathetic to the cause of national defense. When the Wilson administration refused to appropriate sufficient funds for the military, Roosevelt argued that "it becomes the duty of public journals to endeavor to create a public opinion which will both form a policy of National defense and secure from Congress measures for its adoption." By suggesting that intellectuals had a duty to join him in producing a favorable public opinion for their cause, Roosevelt created a coalition among the press and preparedness proponents that he hoped would guarantee the public's consent to preparedness policies. The *New Republic* maintained that the press worked in conjunction with intellectuals to galvanize public opinion. An "anti-German spirit" wrote the editors, "was not less general among writers on magazines and in the newspapers. They popularized what the college professors had been thinking."[10]

PREPAREDNESS ADVOCATES'
USE OF GENDERED LANGUAGE

Heeding Roosevelt's directive, preparedness advocates increased the rate and broadened the magnitude of their activity and propaganda during the early months of 1915, through a steady stream of articles, books, and films designed to play to America's fears of being a weak nation. Hudson Maxim, brother of a machine-gun maker, published *Defenseless America* in which he proclaimed the inevitability of war and predicted that the United States in its present condition would be overrun. As a way of making preparedness seem essential, Maxim used a gendered language — liberally sprinkling his prose with words such as "penetrate" and "invade" — to convey conventional images of a strong manhood ready to protect vulnerable femininity. Utilizing new technology, a moving picture based on the book *The Battle Cry of Peace* capitalized on the ravaged wife and lover to motivate soldiers in training camps.[11]

New defense organizations championed the cause of increasing military defense. In December 1914 the National Security League (NSL) dedicated itself to the task of persuading Congress to increase military appropriations. American democracy, the NSL argued, must aid other democracies in their struggle with autocracy; as a democratic power, America must also defend neutral rights on the seas. By September 1915, twenty-two governors had joined the NSL, giving the organization a broad geographic base of support. Women participated as actively in the preparedness movement as they did in the peace movement. The Women's Section of the Navy League formed in 1915, and various groups had established military training camps for women — which were mostly symbolic rather than functional — by 1916. Then, in December 1915, New York interventionists formed the American Rights Committee, a group consisting of such wealthy men as the owners of the *New York Tribune*. Thus, in both the press and in interest groups, Roosevelt's entreaty to create public opinion was answered.[12]

Politicians could not ignore the change in attitude from neutral passivity to interested activity. As Arthur Link has shown, partisanship played a role in the preparedness movement. "Although the various defense societies had made an honest effort to be nonpartisan," he wrote, "practically all their chief spokesmen were Republicans, associated with the great financial and industrial interests."[13] Republicans used gendered notions of male strength (in contrast to female weakness) to identify the Democratic party as weak on defense, thereby capitalizing on partisan divisions within government to win support.[14]

RELUCTANT PROGRESSIVES SUPPORT PREPAREDNESS

Most progressives initially opposed any increases in government military expenditures or in private corporate arms manufacturing for a number of reasons. The progressives had responded to the European war by noting that it discredited the "military preparedness prevents war" adage.[15] They also assumed war had mainly economic causes and was a form of social disorder: by lending money to industrialists, whose only interest was in winning new markets, bankers were the promoters and beneficiaries of war.[16] Reformers feared that the banks and corporations, which they believed they had succeeded in controlling, would again burst loose during war.[17] Progressives favored an international system based upon compulsory arbitration, the repudiation of war, and therefore, *dis*armament. Yet, between 1915 and 1916, many reformers changed their minds.

Reformers began their "march" toward accepting a military build-up out of a desire to control the politics of preparedness. Order and control, according to the historian Richard McCormick, had made industrialization and big business acceptable, if not palatable, to reformers.[18] Martin applied the progressive desire for order and control to preparedness: "The call for efficiency and the expert was a way . . . of controlling and directing the rate of change in areas of politics, economics, social work." In addition, "pacifists, apart from their opposition to militarism, wanted a proper accounting for the money already expended in the defense budget; a simple, traditional progressive reform which called for the efficient management of public funds."[19]

"REASONABLE" PREPAREDNESS

Rationalizing the arms build-up gave progressives a sense of control. The editors of the *New Republic* articulated this line of thought: "[W]e should regard these super-dreadnoughts as a hideous waste if we did not believe and expect that they can be eventually used by the American government as the instrument of a better understanding among nations, and of the organization of an international system which will diminish the danger and the costs of war."[20] This rationale of "reasonable preparedness" meant that, used for the right purposes, an increase in arms was acceptable. Progressive pacifists within the ranks of the World Peace Foundation, and some members of the Woman's Peace Party, adopted this position.

"REAL" PREPAREDNESS

Meanwhile, another school of thought developed surrounding the preparedness issue. Adherents of "real" preparedness demanded that a program of social upbuilding accompany military increases. During a conference on real preparedness, for example, progressives called for a child labor bill, progressive taxation on large incomes and inheritances, federal acquisition of monopolies, and social insurance against sickness and accident, all of which made militarism more justifiable to reformers. In addition, real preparedness allowed progressives a hand in shaping American military and, concomitantly, economic policy. Preparedness required the adoption of many of the reforms progressives had long been advocating. For example, the efficient mobilization of the nation's resources would require a greater degree of central planning and control of the economy. The progressive publicist William Allen White expressed the sentiments of real preparedness to Roosevelt, saying, "By giving them [American workers] a decent social environment, decent wages, decent treatment as American citizens . . . with all our guns and machinery we may lose any great contest that is forced upon us through a lack of genuine loyalty, of real patriotism, of conviction that this is . . . the fairest country to fight for in the world." The reform-minded editor Paul Kellogg called for "a programme of social and industrial upbuilding, without which as the events in Europe have shown, military preparedness is a thatch of straw."[21]

The progressives' concerns about working-class Americans' level of loyal patriotism, and, by extension, their perceived willingness to fight, reflected anxieties about *male* loyalty, since only men were drafted into the military (women's training camps notwithstanding). The question of *women's* loyalty was not broached by these progressive writers, at least not before the United States actually declared war, nor was the question of women's full participation in the benefits of citizenship during peacetime (i.e., woman suffrage). Suffragists, of course, tried to convince the American public of both: that women's loyalty to the nation *was* relevant and that they were worthy of full inclusion as equal citizens of the United States.

In addition to securing male workers' loyalty, progressives saw preparedness as having intrinsic advantages that would produce a more cohesive society; this, too, was part of real preparedness. The preparedness movement appealed to some progressives as a cure for a national malaise. Roosevelt anticipated these benefits of military preparation. "Throughout the effort to obtain for our country a vertebrate military policy there can be likewise obtained for our people a social efficiency, a discipline, *a sense of international responsibility* that . . . will do much to hasten the day of 'the parliament of man and the federation of the world'" [emphasis added].[22] Real preparedness, along with reasonable preparedness, included a sense of the United States as a model for the rest of the world; the progressive pacifist ideology of internationalism thus became part of the preparedness movement.

Finally, the preparedness movement cultivated a moral imperative to accompany internationalism, which became the final selling point among progressives. By 1916, according to Martin, advocates of preparedness were shifting their concern away from viewing the war as European to presenting it as a Prussian attempt at world domination. "War," wrote Martin, "instead of being evil in itself — a position which pacifist groups felt had attained general acceptance — was shifted in the present case to a war between good and evil."[23] Progressives came to the preparedness camp as its advocates framed the argument in moral terms.[24]

FUNDING OF THE LEAGUE TO ENFORCE PEACE
BY THE WORLD PEACE FOUNDATION

The World Peace Foundation was one pacifist organization that institutionalized internationalism by funding a propreparedness organization and by concomitantly reducing its female-headed programs to educate the public about peace. In June 1915 WPF member Hamilton Holt had conceived of an organization designed to ensure international cooperation: the League to Enforce Peace (LEP). Its members developed a system of arbitration among a federation of nations as a viable way to solve conflict. The league evolved from a seminar of intellectuals held at four organizational dinners. It convened officially at Philadelphia's Independence Hall on Bunker Hill Day, June 17, 1915, a highly publicized effort to emulate the nation's "founding fathers."[25] The only thing missing was a suitable means of funding its program. In July, Harvard president A. Lawrence Lowell outlined the LEP program for members of the World Peace Foundation. All conflicts arising between nations that could not be settled by negotiation would be submitted to a judicial tribunal for hearing and judgment. The disputing countries would jointly use both their economic and military forces against any one of the nations that declared war or committed acts of hostility against one of the other signatory powers.[26]

During discussion, Lowell pointed out that if the United States were to create such a league it would probably have to have more armament — "but not so much more as we shall be obliged to have if the United States does not join such a league."[27] Yet Lowell and his followers presented the program as a new peace initiative and as the best method of opposing excessive preparedness. Former Harvard president Charles W. Eliot supported the LEP with these words, praising the masculine military spirit he saw as part of preparedness:

I am not prepared to oppose distinctly and vigorously the preparedness campaign. There are too many contingencies in the future which may lead us into war; there are too many young Americans who are already thinking it their duty to prepare themselves to be useful as soldiers. *Their motives are lofty and their spirit high*; and I, for one, am not inclined to say to them 'nay' [emphasis added].[28]

But some WPF members wondered how an organization promoting world peace should react to a nation preparing for war. Samuel Elder, for example, expressed the opinion that the foundation was "belligerent to the extent of being willing to fight for peace." A. H. Pillsbury agreed; in his view, the WPF had "a more pressing duty — to oppose the prepared-ness propaganda, which put the U.S. on war footing." Two years later, Pillsbury finally resigned his WPF post because he felt the World Peace Foundation was no longer a peace organization. "I long ago became satis-fied, whatever the merits of the League [to Enforce Peace], that the United States will not enter it [the war] and ought not to," proclaimed Pillsbury. "And because it is plain to me that the remedy for war cannot be more war, and," he added with irony, "that if I held such an opinion I should be . . . disqualified to administer a peace foundation."[29]

The league forced WPF members to review the degree to which they were willing to use force to solve a conflict between nations. To some, such as Pillsbury, the idea that peace could be "enforced" was absurd. The World Peace Foundation divided over the idea but finally voted to support it with a check for $10,000. In conjunction with this move, the foundation reduced the amount of money allocated to the American School Peace League, which effectively removed another woman, program director Fannie Fern Andrews, from the ranks of the WPF.[30]

The LEP proposal, that the United States should establish an international organization compelling countries, by the use of economic and military sanctions, to submit disputes to arbitration, had wide appeal for progressive pacifists. The program not only seemed to provide a way to bring American influence into the international realm but represented, for some who had previously opposed preparedness, a way to reconcile themselves to a limited preparedness program. Hamilton Holt called on both the pacifists and preparedness advocates to rally behind the LEP and forget their differences. A strong and influential America, rather than the particulars of military armaments, became the focal point of the preparedness campaign.[31]

Progressives gradually began shifting away from rejecting preparedness to accepting, in Thompson's words, "a more active idealism" of a strong America.[32] Many progressives, though, did not completely abandon peace, even as they cautiously joined the preparedness movement. The historian Michael A. Lutzker criticized many so-called peace advocates who actually belonged to pacifist societies as well as defense societies. Holt was apparently correct in his opinion that the two sides had little to squabble about. Among female pacifists, for example, the Woman's Peace Party included within its ranks the Coronada, California, Chapter of the Women's Section of the Navy League, a preparedness advocacy group. Two WPP members, Lucia Ames Mead and Elizabeth Glendower Evans, belonged to the LEP. Holt himself founded the LEP but also backed a plan for mediation between belligerents formulated by a University of Wisconsin English professor, Julia Grace Wales.[33]

Members of the WPF who had sharply repudiated the "sentimentalism" of their organization by eliminating some of their women members, and by drawing "respectable" businessmen and lawyers to the fold, were now being drawn into a propreparedness position by the very men whose respectability they had sought. Notwithstanding Pillsbury and Elder, the LEP program *did* seem like a feasible way to keep the respectability the peace movement had gained by allying with men such as Lowell, and to fund an organization that sought international cooperation in time of conflict in order to gain peace. The fact that America would have to incur some military expenditure to "force" the other signatory powers to abide by rulings seemed like a small price to pay. Too, the WPF had been floundering since the death of Edwin Ginn over what direction the organization should take; the LEP program gave the men a chance to feel as though they were actively "working for the principle."[34]

THE ISSUE OF PREPAREDNESS DEBATED
BY THE WOMAN'S PEACE PARTY

At a Woman's Peace Party forum on November 15, 1915, one of the organization's founders, Crystal Eastman, sharply criticized her own organization. She derided the WPP for merely rejecting the European war and then suggested that pacifists bond together against preparedness. She warned that "every congressman will be bombarded with demands for appropriations to finance a big army and navy. On the first day let the Woman's Peace Party have a bill ready calling for a public investigation of the state of our defenses, with a report in three months. Let that be the first plank in our platform."[35] Eastman, too, indicated a need for an active program with a positive ideal.

The impetus behind the creation of the WPP had been to protest against the war, and the women continued, in the months after the war broke out, to try to convince President Wilson to hold a conference of neutral nations to bring an end to the conflict.[36] But two factors turned the women's attention to domestic concerns: the increasing realization that Wilson would not cooperate, or mediate, and the alarming growth of military advocacy in the United States.

In March 1915 Jane Addams addressed the Massachusetts branch of the WPP. Here, she laid out the primary argument against military preparedness that the national WPP would advance in the coming months. "Why spend $45,000,000 for warships, when they will only be reduced to the scrap heap after this war is over?" she asked rhetorically. "We cannot foretell what many of the results of the war will be, but it is certain to mean a limitation of armaments." The preparedness hysteria was unnecessary, in Addams's opinion, because "this country is in no danger of being drawn into war," and wrong in any case because preparedness meant preparing for war. Addams did not suggest that new warships might be used by the United States to bring about world peace.[37]

But the Woman's Peace Party also came to advocate reasonable preparedness, or the view that preparing for war was acceptable under the right circumstances. On November 4, 1915, when Wilson declared his plan to increase the army and boost the amount of money spent on the navy, the WPP wrote a letter to the president, authored by Mead, admitting the necessity of "real preparedness against real dangers" but not "a preposterous preparedness against hypothetical dangers." (The WPP conceded that a nation needed some measure of defense to ensure national sovereignty.) Furthermore, the women argued that preparedness would "create rivalry, suspicion and taxation in every country," and most important of all "would tend to disqualify our National Executive from rendering the epochal service which this world crisis offers for the establishment of permanent peace." Along with other progressives, the WPP expected America to play an active role in international politics.[38]

Preparedness became the chief theme of the first annual convention of the WPP, held in Washington from January 8 to 10, 1916. The most important accomplishment of the conference was the adoption of a congressional program, which the WPP promoted during the coming year. The proposed program focused on the issue of preparedness, which threatened to be the main interest of Congress. The women urged Congress to appoint a joint committee to conduct thorough investigations, with public hearings, and report within the next six months on several matters, including the condition of the U.S. military and naval defenses, with "special reference to the expenditure of past appropriations." This request suggested that *if* the military proved inefficient, then the women might approve further expenditure: in other words, in asking for an investigation, they left themselves open to the possibility of approving a military budget increase. However, the WPP balanced its concern with efficient spending of funds by insisting that an investigation also be made into the "probability of aggressive action by other nations against the U.S. . . . and the possibility of lessening by legislative or diplomatic action the source of friction between this country and other nations."[39]

Further discussion surrounded the question of whether the WPP ought to support two bills concerning armaments, the Crosser and Cummins bills, that were to come before the next legislative session. The Crosser bill called for the elimination of private interest in war by providing government facilities for producing and manufacturing military and naval equipment, while the Cummins bill called more specifically for the government manufacture of armaments. These two bills were understood as antipreparedness legislation because they represented the progressive pacifist drive to take the profit out of war and to control how preparation proceeded.

But the attendees were at odds over whether women had sufficient knowledge of the issues (especially military issues, an area usually considered "man's business") to form an opinion, and by extension, over the exact purpose of their organization. Mrs. Charles Edward Russell spoke for those against endorsing the bill, saying, "I thought the purpose of this congress was to voice our disgust with the abomination of war itself. I think such matters as the code and the technique of war may be very properly left to men." Laura Clay agreed, speaking in sharper terms: "I do not believe we ought to interest ourselves in the manufacture of armaments. . . . I believe we will diminish our influence by undertaking a subject entirely too large and complicated for us. . . . I am sure we are stumbling into dangers of which we know nothing." (Ironically, the timid Clay had earlier made a rousing speech calling for the empowerment of women through suffrage during the 1916 meeting.)[40] Ultimately, the WPP endorsed the Cummins bill but not the Crosser bill.

On the same subject of military funding, the women discussed whether the WPP ought to suggest that Congress vote against increases in arms appropriations. Fanny Garrison Villard took the absolutist stand, as she had earlier on the matter of suffrage, asking to replace the words "no increase" with "no appropriation." Villard articulated the needed principle otherwise lacking in the WPP. She thought that the petition for investigating arms spending, and advocating government-owned munitions plants, had betrayed the true pacifist cause — the resisting of *any* form of militarism, and the need, as Mrs. Russell had noted, "to voice our disgust with war itself."

Countering Villard's request, Rose Forbes declared that it would be impossible to convince anyone in Congress that the government should not appropriate a single dollar for the army and navy; indeed, even most peace workers would not accept such a position.

But Villard persisted. "It seems to me it would be the mission of the Woman's Peace Party to instruct those legislators as to what their duties are towards the matter," she argued. "It matters not what they reply, but it does matter what we say." In other words, Villard posited that the WPP should worry itself not over how others responded to the party but over how women made their voices heard. In rebuttal, Clay voiced the majority sentiment. Her concern was not with the morality of the position but with the pragmatic consequences of the WPP's political reputation: "as we don't want to vote ourselves out of existence, I must disagree. . . . It [the issue of opinions on military appropriations] will have to be left to individual action, and not the Peace Party." Tracy Mygatt objected: "There are many of us in the Peace Party . . . who are waiting for this extreme stand, meaning, if you will, disarmament. . . . there is enough response to that extreme position to make it more than worth our while just from the low ground of expediency to consider it pretty seriously before we turn it away." Still, Villard's proposal to request that the government make no military appropriations was voted down. Pragmatism, like reasonableness, had effectively silenced the opposition.[41]

In its discussion over military issues, the Woman's Peace Party abandoned the moral tones of its original program and platform. In those documents, the pacifists had called upon women to take their stand as "the mother-half of humanity" and "as . . . the custodians of life . . . of the helpless and unfortunate" — in rejecting war and militarism. But in this instance, as would be the case with the party's statement regarding U.S. intervention, the women retreated from their moral stance, which had been delegitimated as unreasonable and not pragmatic. Instead, the women voted to keep the WPP, in Clay's words, "in existence."[42]

ORGANIZATION OF A MIXED-GENDER PEACE GROUP AROUND THE PREPAREDNESS ISSUE

Meanwhile, as the World Peace Foundation voted to finance the League to Enforce Peace, and as the WPP called upon experts to investigate military expenditure, a new peace organization was in the making. On September 20, 1914, within six weeks after the declaration of war, the journalists Paul Kellogg, John Haynes Holmes, Edward Devine, Hamilton Holt, and Frederic Howe allied with the social workers Lillian Wald, Florence Kelley, Julia Lathrop, Jane Addams, and others, to discuss the issue of war in the Henry Street settlement house.[43]

The European war had alarmed the Henry Street group (later the American Union Against Militarism). American relief funds sent overseas threatened to drain financial resources from domestic reforms, and, if the United States should respond to the call for preparedness, money earmarked for reforms would fill military coffers instead. After the war, warned the *Survey*, "social progress would be subordinated to the demands of 'mere social survival.'"[44] The *Survey*, the literary voice of professional social workers, published articles warning against the reversal of reforms already under way. The editors blamed rampant unemployment in Chicago on the war and predicted worsening conditions if the United States were to arm itself.[45]

Foreign policy had not been an issue of importance before 1914 for these reformers, but now the international crisis threatened the progressives' hard-won advances. These social workers, experts in cooperation and mediation among immigrants in multinational neighborhoods, saw themselves as capable of saving the world from war. Instead of calling for experts, Henry Street members looked to their own expertise, a product of their occupations in professional social work and allied fields.[46]

The historian James Martin, too, argued that Henry Street represented a new coalition of progressive pacifists.[47] This may have been so; but the new coalition differed from that of the WPF, which was characterized by hierarchy and domination rather than cooperation. The Henry Street group did not attempt to lure granges, labor unions, or women's organizations into its fold the way the WPF did, although it worked closely with several of those groups. At the same time, the Henry Street members had worked in several different reform organizations. Of the twenty attending the initial meeting, ten wrote articles on social reforms for the *Survey*. Twelve had lived and worked in settlement houses. Eight had been members of the Joint Committee on Industrial Relations. Six were officers or trustees of the National Child Labor Committee, and five had been among the sponsors of a petition to make a special investigation of violations of constitutional rights during the 1913 Paterson strike. The interests of labor figured especially heavily among the reformers.[48]

Membership in the Henry Street group was evenly divided between men and women. Three of the women who were among the founders — Addams, Wald, and Emily Greene Balch — were also members of the Woman's Peace Party. Leadership positions were also divided evenly among women and men. However, women's presences within Henry Street were truncated. Feminist concerns about women's voting rights and labor were not apparent in the organization, nor did it approach pacifism from the standpoint of motherhood, as did the WPP. In this respect, the group offered women further opportunities to work for peace, but such access did not automatically mean that women members used their positions within the group to put forth their feminist agendas. When women in the group spoke, they did not discuss women's issues or speak as feminists. Crystal Eastman (who joined the group later), Addams, and Balch had a great deal to say about suffrage, motherhood, and the relationship of women to war, but they asserted their feminist opinions on those issues when they worked for and represented the Woman's Peace Party.

Neither the men nor the women in Henry Street approached peacemaking with firsthand knowledge of the machinations or intricacies of foreign policy, and, with the notable exception of Addams, they had not been involved in politics abroad. They drew strength from their mutual cooperation with foreigners in settlement houses and their common fear of the deleterious effects of war on domestic reform.[49]

HENRY STREET'S CLASS-BASED
PEACE ADVOCACY

In their repudiation of the older peace organizations, Henry Street members began to tear at the fabric of the progressive class. They had waited — as had the Woman's Peace Party — in vain through the early months of the war for the leaders of the established peace societies, such as the WPF, to act. Holmes criticized the "undemocratic principles and atmosphere" and the exclusivity of "their hand-picked conferences at remote summer resorts" (undoubtedly the Lake Mohonk conferences). Kellogg concurred: "The conservative peace people" had not met the world crisis with any action or message that expressed the "youth and vision of America." Kellogg urged the Henry Street group to launch a national movement and proclaim a bolder, more radical program than that of the old peace societies, an agenda that would "challenge commercialism and commercial exploitation, denounce arms and breathe the spirit of democracy."[50] Holmes, Balch, and Kellogg, through their experience with industrialization and labor, espoused a socialist ideology that blamed a competitive and exploitative economic system for war. Kellogg, for example, warned of a "recrudescence of militarism in America" in the Colorado mining fields, which he compared to the imperialistic practices of absentee capitalism that had caused the war in Europe.[51]

"Toward a Peace that Shall Last," the Henry Street group's manifesto printed in the *Survey*, called for a replacement of the old diplomacy of secrecy and intrigue, of profit takers and back-room deal makers, with a new politics controlled by the people. The reformers heralded their right to speak for the oppressed, a right they had inherited as social workers. "By the unemployed of our water-fronts, and the augmented misery of our cities; by the financial depression which has curtailed our school buildings and crippled our works of good will; by the sluicing of human impulse among us from channels of social development to the back-eddies of salvage and relief — we have a right to speak."[52]

The Henry Street group held contradictory attitudes toward the notion of civilization. On the one hand, it advocated the intermixing of different but equal human groups. On the other hand, it urged the United States and Europe to stop the "predatory exploitation which has embroiled the West and oppressed the East" and to provide an "opportunity for each latent and backward race to build up according to its own genius." Henry Street saw advantages to intermixing, but at the same time it clearly believed that an evolved civilization occupied the West. The West's superiority, however, was being threatened by the present war.[53]

In spite of the socialist leanings of many Henry Street members, they remained confident that President Wilson would soon seek an end to the war. They encouraged him to prohibit the export of all arms and eliminate private profit from arms manufacturers by making munitions a monopoly of the federal government. In accepting preparedness if it meant an end to private profit, Henry Street mirrored the progressive idea of reasonable military preparedness. In advocating social programs alongside preparedness, Addams, Kellogg, and the others supported real preparedness.

On July 20, 1915, Addams met with the pacifists to suggest that bypassing the usual channels of official diplomacy could end the war. This notion sat well with the democratic impulses of the reformers. But at this early stage of the war, their strong, if naive, faith in Wilson would not allow them to agree to a plan they saw as going behind the president's back.[54]

Four months later, however, Wilson himself went behind the backs of his pacifist supporters and announced a program of "reasonable" military preparedness, which included a greatly expanded program of shipbuilding and the creation of a new reserve army of 400,000 men. Progressives, who had remained convinced that Wilson was "one of us," had to conclude that he had surrendered to the militarists. The preparedness issue then became the primary concern of the Henry Street group. The New Yorkers moved their operation to Washington, D.C.; an alteration in name and methods soon followed.

FROM HENRY STREET TO THE AMERICAN UNION AGAINST MILITARISM

In November 1915 the Henry Street group renamed itself the Anti-"Preparedness" Committee; in January 1916 it became the American Union Against Militarism (AUAM), reflecting the specific goals of the organization: to "throw . . . a monkey wrench into the machinery of preparedness," and to "stop the war" through a conference of neutrals.[55]

THE AUAM'S METHODOLOGY: DIALOGUE

The AUAM's method became one of constantly seeking a dialogue with its opposition, a tactic the editor Paul Kellogg developed in the pages of his journal the *Survey*. Members followed Wilson's "Swing Around the Circle for Preparedness," the president's January 1916 campaign advocating a stronger military. When Wilson challenged his opponents to rent their own speaking facilities and state their case to the public, the union did exactly that, launching an eleven-city speaking tour called the "Truth About Preparedness."

Amos Pinchot's harsh analysis of the class interests of the preparedness movement set the tone of the "Truth" tour. He blasted "superficial reformers" Roosevelt and Elihu Root for their class-based criticism of American society. Pinchot criticized Root's statement that "the principles of American liberty today stand in need of a renewed devotion. . . . [Americans] have grown so rich, we have lived in ease and comfort and peace so long, that we have forgotten what we owe to those agreeable incidents of life."[56] Root and other "distinguished leaders," Pinchot charged, were judging the nation by the prosperity of a few. Pinchot clearly marked the AUAM as an organization devoted to promote ordinary people over the extraordinary wealth of a few.[57]

In addition to answering the challenge of its opponents, the AUAM made other efforts to start a dialogue on the subject of preparedness, and to counter the monologic strategies of military advocates. For example, members published a pamphlet that provided readers with *both sides* of the military training issue (see Figure 3.1). In response to visual propaganda for preparedness, the AUAM proved itself one of the most creative groups within the American peace movement. To counter military symbols, such as Uncle Sam, glorified male soldiers, and victimized women, the AUAM "enlisted" a parrot, named General Wood after the preparedness campaign's most ardent and highly decorated soldier, which shrieked "Prepare!" to all who entered the AUAM office. The organization's mascot was a huge papier-mâché sword-wielding dinosaur, suggesting the backwardness of the preparedness campaign. Masters of satire, the group designed a twenty-two–cartoon poster exhibit called "War Against War," a needling of "superficial reformers," among others, in cartoon form.[58]

The union's primary function was to act as a nationwide press service oriented toward influencing Congress. Publicity director Charles Hallinan sent out descriptions of the AUAM's lobbying efforts relative to specific congressional hearings and legislation across the nation. But in its work with Congress the group lost some of its potency for radical reform. Rather than blocking increased military expenditure in Congress, the AUAM merely succeeded in watering down preparedness bills. The union had lobbied to stop any increase in naval appropriations, but when this effort proved unsuccessful, they worked to have the Hensley clause attached to the Naval Appropriations bill. The provision authorized and requested the president to invite the heads of states of belligerent governments to a conference at the end of the war to plan for a court of arbitration and to consider disarmament. The president would be authorized to appoint citizens to represent the United States, appropriating money to pay them. Words such as "request," "authorize," and "invite" hardly heralded the beginning of democratic control of foreign policy.[59]

FIGURE 3.1

Universal Military Training
A Debate:
Henry L. West v. *Charles T. Hallinan*

of the

of the

National
Security
League

American Union
Against
Militarism

"God help us if we should prove as weak as we are rich!"
—Mr. West, p. 4.

Source: Records of the American Union Against Militarism, Swarthmore College Peace Collection.

In essence, the AUAM became trapped by relying solely on its class-based analysis. The group proved too willing to accept preparedness if the money for it were procured in a more egalitarian fashion. AUAM members wanted Congress to impose income and inheritance taxes to meet the costs of any increased military expenditures, and the 1916 Revenue Act did not disappoint them. In a taunting statement mirroring the views of the AUAM and other antimilitarists, Congressman Warren Worth Bailey (D-Pennsylvania) asked: "Where are the members of the Preparedness league and the Navy league? In the counting room hollering loud and long because they find that their incomes must bear a portion of the burden they had hoped to unload upon the farmer and the steel worker."[60]

The union saw foreign and domestic policy in terms of the people versus the government elites who claimed the right to speak on behalf of the masses. The logic of the union, as the historian C. Roland Marchand has written, went something like this: "If the common people of the nation . . . opposed preparedness and sought a mediated end to the war, then a government that failed to take action in accordance with their desires must be under the sway of groups employing it against majority interests."[61] Preparedness advocates worked to create public sympathy for militarism, which then resulted in the compliance of Wilson and enough progressives in government to produce a preparedness program acceptable to progressives. The AUAM charged an upper-class controlled press with fomenting war, in effect undermining the notion that the preparedness movement was in the interests of a democratic nation.

The historian Ralph Nafziger denied later that newspapers constituted a "fourth estate" during the war. He belittled the notion that the press was on par with bankers and munitions makers as determining factors that caused the United States to prepare for, and ultimately to enter, the war. Certainly, the New York papers strongly advocated preparedness. But papers such as the *San Francisco Chronicle* and the *Christian Science Monitor* did not support the policy. Furthermore, focus on the 1916 election took attention away from events overseas, lulling the public into seeing preparedness as an isolationist move to secure the United States' neutrality, rather than as a move toward war.[62]

Perhaps more significant, according to Nafziger, was the growing partisanship during the 1916 campaign of newspapers claiming that Wilson's Democratic Party was "soft" on defense. Nafziger's analysis implied that gendered notions of strength and weakness played a role in the preparedness campaign. Indeed, insisting that a president, and a nation, avoid the charge of weakness was a fundamental part of the rhetoric surrounding the issue of militarism. (Congressional representatives, speaking in favor of preparedness, and ultimately of U.S. intervention, imbued their speeches with images of white manhood, strength, and military glory.)

In blaming preparedness on a conspiracy between a monolithic press and the upper class, the AUAM apparently lumped all papers into the same category as the New York press. Yet the union itself contributed frequently to news about preparedness in the weekly press releases that Hallinan sent to papers nationwide. Furthermore, as so many of its members either owned or worked for magazines, such as the *Survey*, they clearly had access to the print media that many other interest groups did not have. More harmful, the charge that their enemies conspired against them took their attention away from making a more constructive analysis of their own shortcomings and of the preparedness movement's base of strength.

The multitude of defense councils and leagues that sprang to life in favor of militarism revealed how the active consent of the public was obtained by the dominant class. Marching through city streets, defense-minded patriots prepared the United States for intervention in the European war by framing the issue as one of peace through strength: in other words, the United States needed a strong defense if it was to remain democratic and avoid invasion by warring nations. Meanwhile, the "peace through strength" adage delegitimated the idea of peace through moral sentiment, on which the AUAM had based its original manifesto and on which the WPP had grounded its feminist pacifist ideology. The numerous preparedness parades and organizations gave people the sense of involvement in a democratic movement that formed part of the consent that reaffirmed hegemonic rule of the elite.[63] The AUAM put forth the most active campaign on behalf of pacifism to counter preparedness, but beyond encouraging citizens to write to their congressional representatives, it did not offer people the active involvement that the preparedness advocates did.

The AUAM was good at criticizing the enemy but bad at gathering support for its cause. The union realized that preparedness allowed the munitions industries to line their pockets and that government and industry were conspiring to involve the United States in the war. Union members were also aware that preparedness was the government's way of creating public opinion sympathetic to actual military intervention before it occurred. But they failed to take the last step in threatening the power of the dominant class. They did not follow through on their initial moral imperative as issued in the "Toward a Peace That Shall Last" manifesto. The union concerned itself too much with seeking government ownership of munitions industries and arguing for more equitable taxes to pay for the arms build-up than with insisting that there be no increase in military spending *at all*. In compromising on the issue, the AUAM also weakened its moral imperative.

The issue of military preparedness, steeped in gendered notions of masculine strength, undermined the unity of the progressive class. On the one hand were elitists, including a majority of members within the World Peace Foundation and the Woman's Peace Party, who insisted on controlling the course of preparedness by investigating the mismanagement of military expenditure and then by accepting increases in the armed forces and armaments in the name of peace — thereby awaiting the social benefits they thought the nation would derive from preparedness. On the other hand were members of the American Union Against Militarism, who thought that money spent on the military would take money away from needed domestic reforms; because they saw a conspiracy between munitions makers, the press, and military advocates in government, they saw preparedness as undemocratic. The AUAM hailed the 1916 Revenue Act as forcing the upper classes to pay for increased military spending, and in this respect, the union, too, came to accept preparedness. But in focusing on class differences, they ignored the way preparedness advocates gathered public support by evoking a need for military strength to "combat" a national military "impotence." The divisions within the progressive class over preparedness continued into the debate over U.S. intervention in the war in 1917.

NOTES

1. Gail Bederman, *Manliness and Civilization: A Cultural History of Gender and Race in the United States, 1880–1917* (Chicago: University of Chicago Press, 1995), 23–25; Edward Devine quoted in *Paul U. Kellogg and the Survey: Voices for Social Welfare and Social Justice*, by Clarke A. Chambers (Minneapolis: University of Minnesota Press, 1971), 52.

2. Bederman, *Manliness*, 6–7; David Starr Jordan, "An Indictment by David Starr Jordan, Chancellor of Stanford University," undated, SR 12.2, WPP Papers, SCPC.

3. Arthur S. Link, *Woodrow Wilson and the Progressive Era* (New York: Harper, 1954), 177. See his chapter, "Preparedness Controversy, 1914–1916," 174–196.

4. James Parker Martin, "The American Peace Movement and the Progressive Era, 1910–1917," (Ph.D. diss., Rice University, 1975), 243. Martin cites two articles written about preparedness before June 1914, one in *McClure's* and one in *Scientific American*.

5. Martin, "American Peace Movement," 244–245.

6. John A. Thompson, *Reformers and War: American Progressive Publicists and the First World War* (Cambridge: Cambridge University Press, 1987), 127.

7. Theodore Roosevelt, "Democracy and Military Preparation: The Ideal," *Outlook*, 25 November 1914, 664. The series continued in the 9, 16, and 30 December 1914 issues. Gail Bederman, in *Manliness*, devotes chapter 5 to TR's foreign policy and his concept of civilization.

8. Thompson, *Reformers*, 127; Martin also discusses the propreparedness strategies, albeit less thoroughly than Thompson. See Martin, "American Peace Movement," 244.

9. Walter L. Adamson, *Hegemony and Revolution: A Study of Antonio Gramsci's Political and Cultural Theory* (Berkeley: University of California Press, 1980), 171.

10. Theodore Roosevelt, "The Army for a Democracy," *Outlook*, 30 December 1914, 988; See Antonio Gramsci, *Selections from the Prison Notebooks*, ed. and trans. Quintin Hoare and Geoffrey Nowell-Smith (New York: International Publishers, 1971), 148–149, and 195–196 for Gramsci's analysis of the press's role in the hegemonic process; "Who Willed American Participation?" New Republic, 14 April 1917, 308.

11. Link, Woodrow Wilson, 178; see Neil A. Wynn, *From Progressivism to Prosperity: World War I and American Society* (New York: Holmes and Meier, 1986), 32; Hudson Maxim, *Defenseless America* (New York: Hearst's International Library Co., 1915), vii–viii, xvi; Martin, "American Peace Movement," 295.

12. Link, *Woodrow Wilson*, 177, 176; Barbara Steinson, *American Women's Activism in World War I* (New York: Garland Press, 1982), 192–199 describes the women's military training camps; Wynn, *From Progressivism to Prosperity*, 135.

13. Link, *Woodrow Wilson*, 179.

14. Partisan lines were not always clear, however. Martin cites Senator Moses H. Clapp's Memorial Day address as the best articulation of antipreparedness sentiment; Clapp was a Republican. See Martin, "American Peace Movement," 252.

15. *Independent*, 17 August 1914, 228.

16. Link, *Woodrow Wilson*, 180.

17. Martin, "American Peace Movement," 253.

18. Richard L. McCormick, "The Discovery that 'Business Corrupts Politics': A Reappraisal of Progressivism," *American Historical Review*, 86 (1981): 247–274.

19. Martin, "American Peace Movement," 22, 267.

20. *New Republic* quoted in *Reformers*, by Thompson, 134.

21. White and Kellogg quoted in *Reformers*, by Thompson, 139, 140.

22.   Roosevelt, "Democracy and Military Preparation," 665, emphasis added; TR quoted George Washington here.

23.   Martin, "American Peace Movement," 244.

24.   Woodrow Wilson framed his preparedness program around this argument, which became the premise of his war declaration. See Michael Lutzker, "The Pacifist as Militarist: a Critique of the American Peace Movement, 1898–1914," *Societas* 5 (Spring 1975): 103.

25.   Martin, "American Peace Movement," 136.

26.   "Minutes of a Board of Trustees Meeting," 25 July 1915, DG 55, Box 2, WPF Papers, SCPC.

27.   Ibid.

28.   Charles Eliot to Edward Cummings, 15 July 1915, DG 55, Box 5, WPF Papers, SCPC.

29.   Ibid.; A. E. Pillsbury to George A. Plimpton, 6 April 1917, DG 55, Box 5, WPF Papers, SCPC.

30.   Martin describes the upheaval in the WPF's funding of the American School Peace League, its main education program, in "American Peace Movement," 140–142.

31.   Thompson, *Reformers*, 135.

32.   Ibid.

33.   Lutzker, "Pacifist as Militarist"; WPP membership lists, SR 12.1, WPP Papers, SCPC; Steinson describes the Wales plan of continuous mediation and Holt's backing of it in *American Women's Activism*, 53.

34.   Thompson uses this phrase to describe the shift from pacifism to limited preparedness, in *Reformers*, 135.

35.   Eastman quoted in *A History of the Woman's Peace Party*, by Marie Louise Degen (1939; reprint, New York: Garland Press, 1972), 154.

36.   Both the WPF and the American Union supported this idea; Martin, "American Peace Movement," 176–178, discussed the conference and how its advocates tried to win Wilson's support.

37.   Quoted in *History*, by Degen, 152.

38.   Ibid., 153.

39.   Ibid., 160. Crystal Eastman wanted to ensure that America was getting "better defense for our money," Steinson, *American Women's Activism*, 126.

40.   "Annual Meeting, January 1916, minutes," sessions 1–5, SR 12.1, WPP Papers, SCPC. See Clay's speech (abridged) the same.

41.   Ibid.

42.   "Preamble and Platform" 10 January 1915; amended 11 January 1916; SR 12.1, WPP Papers, SCPC.

43.   Hamilton Holt belonged to both the more radical Henry Street group (later the AUAM) and the conservative WPF. It was his opinion that both sides of the preparedness issue could come together. For an explanation of his allegiances, see Warren F. Kuehl, *Hamilton Holt: Journalist, Internationalist, Educator* (Gainesville: University of Florida Press, 1980), 111.

44.   *Survey*, 26 September 1914, 629–630.

45.   *Survey*, 26 December 1914, 336.

46.   C. Roland Marchand, *The American Peace Movement and Social Reform, 1898–1918* (Princeton, N.J.: Princeton University Press, 1972), 225.

47.   Martin, "American Peace Movement," 262.

48.   Marchand, *American Peace Movement*, 225, 226, 228.

49.   Ibid., 225–226.

50.   Ibid., 227. The WPP also communicated frustration with older peace societies, see chapter 2.

51.   Kellogg quoted in *American Peace Movement*, by Marchand, 234.

52.   *Survey*, 17 April 1915, 72. This piece contained the same emotional plea for wartorn Europe as the WPP expressed in its preamble, though it addressed women only as victims of war.

53.   Marchand, *American Peace Movement*, 228.

54.   Steinson, *American Women's Activism*, 161.

55.   Marchand, *American Peace Movement*, 241–242.

56.   Clarke A. Chambers, *Paul U. Kellogg and the Survey: Voices for Social Welfare and Social Justice* (Minneapolis: University of Minnesota Press, 1971), 59–60, describes an incident where Kellogg had used the pages of the *Survey* to put forth his ideas about intervention; he then offered to give the pro-interventionist side a chance to express its views; Amos Pinchot, "America and the Real Preparedness," manuscript of speech, reel 10.2, AUAM Papers, SCPC.

57.   For details about the tour, see Blanche Weisen Cook, "Woodrow Wilson and the Anti-Militarists, 1914–1918," (Ph.D. diss., Johns Hopkins University, 1970), 63–67. Crystal Eastman and Mary Ware Dennett planned and organized the tour, although none of the women in the AUAM were among the speakers.

58.   Reel 10.2, AUAM Papers, SCPC, includes the debate; for preparedness posters see Walton Rawls, *Wake Up America!: World War I and the American Poster* (New York: Abbeville Press, 1988); many of the posters in the "War Against War" campaign are in the Swarthmore College Peace Collection.

59.   Martin, "American Peace Movement," 261. An assessment of activities of the preceding year can be found in "Program for 1917," reel 10.2, AUAM Papers, SCPC.

60.   Bailey quoted in *Woodrow Wilson*, by Link, 196.

61.   Marchand, *American Peace Movement*, 244.

62.   Ralph O. Nafziger, "The American Press and Public Opinion and the World War, 1914–April 1917," (Ph.D. diss., University of Wisconsin, 1938), 455, 400, 403.

63.   Roger Simon, *Gramsci's Political Thought: An Introduction* (London: Lawrence and Wishart, 1982), 62. Simon provides examples of ruling classes that activated popular feelings of nationalism and patriotism in diverse situations and societies.

4

Doing "Our Plain Duty": The Congressional Debate and the Pacifist Voice

Just as the peace movement reached its height of popularity among progressive reformers, the nation's lawmakers plunged the United States into war. As the peace historian Charles DeBenedetti has shown, America's involvement in World War I simultaneously fulfilled and ruptured the progressive movement.[1] After helping to create a war emergency the government responded with the kind of social programs progressives had long supported, such as regulating industrial production to meet national needs. Moreover, intervention in the war helped realize progressive reforms, such as elevating the position of organized labor and hastening the passage of Prohibition and woman suffrage. All of these moves were designed to secure public consent to the government's wartime policies.

At the same time, U.S. intervention in the European conflict led to the fragmentation of progressive coalitions. Within the Woman's Peace Party (WPP), for example, the Massachusetts branch pledged loyalty to the president, while the U.S. government accused the New York City branch of being disloyal to Wilson. When intervention appeared imminent, radical newcomers to the American Union Against Militarism (AUAM) formed a Conscientious Objector's Bureau to aid dissidents, while the group's founders promised to comply with the government's prosecution of the war. A majority of progressives within the peace movement withdrew from activism, while the more radical members, especially feminist and socialist agitators, continued to protest U.S. intervention. Feminist pacifists, and socialists of both sexes, formed a new group, the Emergency Peace Federation (EPF). The radicals' attempts to stop the war declaration in Congress became a test of the peace movement's influence in American government.[2]

But most lawmakers debating the war declaration found the pacifists' appeals unpersuasive. Instead, the majority of representatives voted for intervention. Their votes were implicitly and explicitly gendered, and at times race biased, reflecting concerns about rebuilding an honorable, white, male-dominated nation. Moreover, noninterventionists shared their opponents' concerns.

Even while progressive coalitions were breaking down during the controversy over intervention, progressive ideology persisted. Pro-war progressives articulated their stance in the movement's terms, helping more cautious progressives "ease the way to war."[3] By adopting the progressive ideology of internationalism, hawkish congressmen obtained most progressives' consent to military intervention. While progressive men envisioned a nation built on a strengthened manhood to prosecute the war, female progressives called upon American women, whom they believed still desired peace, to keep the country out of the war. But because congressional arguments for war were successfully made in masculinist terms, in some respects the women's strategy served only to confirm that victory, especially when they argued for peace in ways that depicted women as the exclusive moral bearers of pacifism.

PRO- AND ANTI-INTERVENTIONISTS WITHIN THE PROGRESSIVE CLASS

As tensions developed between the United States and the warring nations, progressives debated the prospect of U.S. intervention. Those opposing belligerency felt that American security was not really at risk in the European war and that intervention would merely serve to line the pockets of munitions makers. AUAM member Paul Kellogg expressed the first part of this formula. The question of intervention, he wrote, "has to do with the defence of American rights — of American lives and American ships — on the high seas," and because the European war was not yet "a clear case of struggle between democracy and Prussianism," he could not support intervention. David Starr Jordan, who resigned from the World Peace Foundation (WPF) to assist the AUAM, and still later joined the Emergency Peace Federation, attacked the "New York brokers" and "Boston tories," charging that the war was a deliberate "backfire against democracy."[4] Finally, the AUAM's Amos Pinchot insisted that U.S.

democracy depended on nonintervention: "If we are to have [a] democracy . . . worth living in, some nation, for the sake of these things and in the name of a stricken world, must be human enough . . . to say 'this thing shall spread no further,'" argued Pinchot. "No talk about commercial losses or gains is tolerable at this time of the world's necessity."[5]

But pro-interventionists also argued on behalf of democracy, explaining that U.S. involvement might bring about a democratic Europe and increased government regulation at home, arguments that reinforced progressive hegemony. Progressives in this camp viewed intervention in the same way they perceived real preparedness: as an opportunity to reform the nation in progressive terms. The *New Republic*, for example, urged progressives to work for government regulation of production, prices, and profits; improvement of labor conditions; and the immediate conscription of income to pay for U.S. belligerency, which the editors already saw as a foregone conclusion a week before the actual declaration.[6] Furthermore, pro-interventionists *did* see American rights as worth the price of U.S. belligerency. American involvement would rid the world of the enemy, which they had come to see as Prussianism. "While this spirit of lawlessness and frightfulness is abroad in the world, the United States should oppose it with all the force at its command," declared the *Independent*, voice of the WPF and its beneficiary, the LEP. "The battle we wage is for a far greater cause than the vindication of national honor or the defense of our national rights. We shall fight to overthrow an implacable *enemy of humanity*, an unrelenting menace to democracy" (italics added).[7] Clearly, in creating an enemy — a nonhuman "Hun" — the interventionists advanced their ability to obtain public approval of war. War posters (see Figure 4.1) helped Americans visualize the foe as a fiendish menace that threatened the nation's vulnerable women.

On one issue nearly all progressives were united: they expected U.S. intervention to pose a threat to civil liberties. On this point, the AUAM made its most lasting mark on American society when it created the Civil Liberties Bureau. Even the interventionist *New Republic* acknowledged that "war always brings with it a tendency to intolerance" and advocated the formation of an organization to protect freedom of speech.[8]

But in the end, as U.S. belligerency became fact rather than speculation, most progressives came to support the war. Even Kellogg and Pinchot ceased opposition as soon as America entered the conflict.[9] Scholars have proposed various interpretations of the progressives' capitulation to intervention. The historian John Thompson offered three reasons for the progressives' gradual acceptance of U.S. involvement in

FIGURE 4.1

Source: *Beat Back the Hun*, World War I Liberty Bond Poster, C. 1918, Fred Strothmann, artist. Gift of John W. Campbell to the Museum of the City of New York.

the war. First, progressives maintained their faith in President Wilson. Even the AUAM, whose members had heckled Wilson during his preparedness campaign, thought that "the president would handle the international situation at least as wisely as Congress."[10] Second, progressives desired to play a part in the momentous event — the "Great War" — of their time. Finally, Thompson insisted that a weakening of the progressives' status within public life caused them to advocate intervention. Progressives were "eager to cultivate personal relationships with those in power," an attitude that Thompson interpreted as revealing "a loss of confidence in their importance as spokesmen for a substantial section of public opinion."[11] He interpreted the decision to enter the war as part of a public arena where real power resided, thus conflating war with social and political power, and leaving the private musings of progressive publicists out of his scholarship. This public-private dichotomy aided in the construction of hegemonic power. If war were solely a matter of public policy, then politicians could dismiss the peace movement, especially the women's peace movement, to the feminine, private — and therefore, irrelevant — domain.

GENDER AND THE PRO-WAR ARGUMENT: THE ATTRACTION OF MALE COMRADESHIP

Thompson overlooked another important point, however. The desire to participate in the war certainly affected both interventionists and noninterventionists. Hamilton Holt, editor of *Independent* and WPF member, toured the Western front in February 1917, and "in a spirit which would have shocked his pacifist friends," wrote Holt's biographer, "stopped to fire a shell at the Germans." Even AUAM member Edward Devine envied European belligerents for their fighting spirit. "The fellowship of armies, of the hospitals, of the prison camps prophesies a new and better social order," he wrote. "We who hate war . . . hope . . . the good Lord will deliver us from the evils of selfishness, sordidness, slothfulness, pettiness of soul" that characterized peacetime.[12] But "selfishness, slothfulness, and pettiness of soul" hardly described those pacifists who continued to work actively for peace. Progressives who moved into the interventionist camp did not do so because the peace movement had become slothful. Instead, Devine and others yearned wistfully for a *male* comradeship that they believed the progressive peace movement did not offer. Propaganda posters depicting the comradeship of army life were designed to attract young men into the service.

THE USE OF PROGRESSIVE
IDEOLOGY TO ADVOCATE WAR

When Thompson wrote that reformers came to advocate intervention because progressivism had lost status, he missed another significant point. President Wilson proposed intervention in progressive terms. "One can examine scores of speeches by . . . [progressive] peace advocates," wrote the historian Michael A. Lutzker, "only to come to the dismaying conclusion that they were, in effect, preparing the groundwork for Woodrow Wilson's leadership in the war to end all wars."[13] Wilson's use of the progressive ideology of internationalism signaled greater public acceptance of progressivism, not less. As the government successfully presented belligerency in progressive terms, progressive members of the AUAM and the WPP retreated from peace activism, leaving the peace movement, as Emily Greene Balch noted, in the hands of the pacifists.[14]

The progressives' standpoints on intervention depended, in part, on their analyses of the European nations at war. "Events in Europe," wrote Arthur Link, "conspired to make continued American neutrality difficult, if not impossible." The two major powers — Britain and Germany — were preparing a bid for total victory, and "to preserve neutrality in the face of such assault would be nearly impossible at best." But Link went too far in attributing the cause of American belligerency to European action. He assumed a monolithic American public in which citizens "preferred to abandon their rights on the seas rather than go to war to defend them."[15] But the path the United States followed to intervention revealed how Wilson shaped his position on war to persuade the American public, and Congress, that the world needed a strong democracy to combat autocracy in Europe.

In his speech to Congress on 22 January 1917, President Wilson insisted that a just and lasting peace could not prevail without American assistance. "Peace," he proclaimed, using the language of the pacifist progressives, "must satisfy the principles of American government. . . . The equality of nations, upon which peace must be founded, if it is to last, must be an equality of rights."[16] Wilson offered American assistance in helping to find a lasting peace through the extension of democratic principles abroad. He wanted to negotiate an end to the war but only under his conditions: a pro-Allies settlement that he himself would shape. Thus, U.S. peace activists' rhetoric played directly into President Wilson's hands: they had argued for a conference of neutral nations and for the establishment of an international organization after the war, headed by an American elite.

By early February, however, events turned against both the president and the pacifists. Berlin sensed imminent U.S. intervention after Britain rebuffed Germany's willingness to negotiate peace. In response, Germany resumed unrestricted submarine warfare. Wilson angrily retaliated by severing diplomatic relations with Berlin. Then, on 24 February, the British government passed on to Wilson the intercepted text of a telegram from the German foreign minister, Alfred Zimmermann, and the German ambassador to Mexico, proposing an alliance with Mexico if the United States should intervene, in exchange for German assistance in retrieving for Mexico lost territory in Texas, New Mexico, and Arizona. Wilson released the telegram to the press, and an uproar ensued. Here was a specific threat to U.S. citizens and property in the Southwest. Instead of plunging directly into war, however, the commander-in-chief placated pacifists by asking Congress to authorize a policy of "armed neutrality" (using force to protect rights directly threatened by the submarine campaign but not entering the war on the side of the Allies), an idea proposed by AUAM member Carlton J. Hayes.[17] When Senator Robert M. La Follette (R-Wisconsin) successfully filibustered the bill, Wilson found a loophole that allowed him to arm ships without congressional authorization.

In March 1917 another event occurred that made the notion of U.S. intervention more acceptable to progressive pacifists. Revolutionaries in Russia threw off the chains of monarchy. Now, all the Allied forces had constitutionally based democracies. The thought of fighting with the Allies suddenly became more palatable to progressives within the World Peace Foundation, the Woman's Peace Party, and the American Union Against Militarism. Each of these organizations, however, had different reasons for capitulating to war, outlined below.

THE WORLD PEACE FOUNDATION
FOR INTERVENTION

Members of the World Peace Foundation and their beneficiaries, the League to Enforce Peace (LEP), accepted Wilson's reasons for intervention. The LEP's understanding of the European war coincided with Wilson's 22 January "Peace Without Victory" speech and with his War Message. The league, which had been formed in the wake of the preparedness movement, represented the "culmination of the dream of the eventual imposition of order upon the world by the 'civilized nations,'" according to the historian James P. Martin. "Peace and justice were to be guaranteed by American principles."[18] The *Independent* saw U.S. entry as the only way to stop the European war. The journal forecast American intervention in terms of the progressive concept of internationalism. "We shall have entered the war in order to maintain our inalienable right to live at peace and unmolested in the sisterhood of nations. . . . We must fight only to get peace, universal, durable, guaranteed."[19] Members saw in the possibility of U.S. intervention an opportunity to put an American elite at the front of the international government it sought to design. Supporting the Allies from the beginning of the war, the LEP saw U.S. intervention as a way to ensure Allied victory.

The league chose to side with the powerful elite in the U.S. government by endorsing Wilson's cautious move toward war and concomitantly by wooing the administration's more eager interventionists. To this end, the members changed their letterhead. Previously, the words "League to Enforce Peace" were positioned with equal emphasis across the page; now, the organization began printing the word "enforce" on its stationery in blood red letters.[20]

THE WOMAN'S PEACE PARTY
DIVIDED OVER INTERVENTION

Also representative of this conservative wing of the peace movement in early 1917 was the Massachusetts branch of the Woman's Peace Party. Since the WPP allowed its local branches nearly complete autonomy, they developed and disseminated policies and programs that sometimes differed from the WPP's national executive board. The Massachusetts branch often reacted negatively to national board statements, while also actively developing and publicizing its own rhetoric.

Five members of the Massachusetts branch's executive board articulated their position in a statement to other members and to the organization's national directors. President Wilson, contended the women, was firmly committed to the abolition of war. Even as the group's leaders retained their conviction that war must end forever, in the same breath they approved of U.S. intervention in the current conflict. They were convinced that the United States ought to continue fighting until it had nullified the possibility of "world domination by any imperialistic autocracy." Indicating their support for Wilson, they stated "that in taking up arms against the German government the United States is fighting to dethrone a tyranny that threatens, in the words of the President, 'to master and debase men everywhere.'"[21] According to this logic, an enemy who is "everywhere" must be met with an equally omnipresent military force. The Massachusetts branch deferred to "statesmanship" in any way necessary to defeat Germany. Furthermore, the women believed that this war would be the last, and that it would make the world "safe for democracy." Finally, in sacrificial language they pledged their willingness to "bear a contemporary curtailment of our freedom for the ultimate realization of world freedom."[22]

The rhetoric of the national Woman's Peace Party differed only subtly in tone from that of the Massachusetts branch. The executive board met on 21 February 1917 to hammer out a statement concerning the possibility of U.S. intervention. These pacifist suffragists were not willing simply to concede power to Wilson or to Congress; rather, the national WPP sought an avenue to political power. To obtain access to it, the women fashioned a statement that anticipated the legalistic commitment to rights that would dominate the debate in Congress two months later, while also advocating progressive internationalism. The women believed that the war would result in the establishment of an international tribunal to oversee the rights of passengers to travel upon the high seas. Furthermore, the war offered the United States an opportunity to show its adherence to internationalism. The women *"respectfully remind*[ed] our government of arbitration treaties . . . [we] would *earnestly beg* that the President and Congress . . . secure the legal settlement of all difficulties in which our nation may be involved." Finally, the women declared, "We hold that the difficulty arising between the United States and Germany does not affect the duty of the greatest neutral nation to do all that can be done to help . . . find a basis for a just and stable peace at the earliest possible moment" (emphasis added).[23]

The leadership of the national WPP contended that intervention was primarily a legal issue, and that the United States, as a superior nation, had a duty to "help" (meaning implicitly to "intervene" in behalf of) the belligerent nations. The language used by the women contrasted starkly with their 1915 preamble and program. In 1917 the WPP did not discuss women's place in politics, or mothers' special interest in abolishing war, or a woman's moral revulsion at the use of violence to end conflict.

The implicit endorsement of U.S. intervention, replete with patriotic sentiment and opportunities for women to participate in the war effort, contradicted the Massachusetts branch of the WPP's pledge to work for peace. The women confirmed their loyalty to the president and his authority by locating political power firmly in the executive's hands and (considering the Massachusetts women's repudiation of suffrage and other forms of direct participation by women) in the hands of men. Their loyalty in the face of intervention perpetuated their belief in male domination. While they approved of the notion that women, as mothers, had an interest in peace, they did not translate that interest into political power.

The national WPP, by contrast, wanted to participate in government. These women backed off from their earlier rhetoric of "women's special interests" because, as suffragists, they wanted to gain legitimacy in the eyes of a male government they hoped would grant women the vote in the coming legislative term. As the United States prepared to enter war, the WPP, to gain public approval, adopted the government's language of legalistic concerns. Undoubtedly, the national WPP continued to hope for peace; but the public statements they issued also revealed a distinct change in strategy. Whereas at the group's founding the women argued from the standpoint of gender difference, they now focused on women's equality relative to men.

DISSOLUTION OF THE AUAM

Meanwhile, the American Union Against Militarism wrote its own response to U.S. intervention. Initially, the group raised a series of piercing questions: Was the U.S. government's purpose to maintain the British Empire? Or was it to change the government of Germany by force? Extending their class-based interpretation of the preparedness issue to the realm of intervention, the pacifists asked what Wilson meant by "fighting for democracy," when leadership resided with such aristocrats as former Secretary of War Elihu Root and the multimillionaire financier J. P. Morgan, neither of whom represented "the people." Finally, asked the AUAM, "How do we [Americans] make democracy safe by adopting the methods of tyranny? . . . Who are we to act as judge, jury and executioner?"[24] The AUAM sharply questioned the United States' purpose in intervening in the war.

Paul Kellogg's 17 February *Survey* article reflected what became the majority opinion of his organization: that protection of American shipping rights was not a sufficient reason to intervene and that the evil of "Prussianism" was not exclusive to Germany. Kellogg described Prussianism as an isolated form of nationalism that relied on force as its method for maintaining a nation's rights and its security. "I find this true not alone of Germany," wrote Kellogg, "I find it true of our own psychology in this national crisis. . . . I am not for going into the war to throttle Prussianism, because I cannot bring myself to believe it can be done that way." However, Kellogg approved of Wilson's repudiation of "Prussian-ism" and of armed neutrality: "I unreservedly approve of President Wilson's course in breaking diplomatic relations with Germany. . . . His act was a moral condemnation in the courts of mankind . . . and in that condemnation he has the country with him."[25] Kellogg's loyalty to Wilson would prove a stronger sentiment than his reluctance to intervene.

The AUAM was not as conciliatory when it came to congressional restrictions on civil liberties. On 14 February 1917 Congress passed the Threats Against the President Act, making it treasonous to harm the pres-ident. This act proved that the progressives' concern with freedom of speech was not unfounded. As Kellogg wrote, "The day war is declared, that day we are invaded — our liberties, our reason, our power to choose for ourselves [will be compromised]."[26] Among pacifists such as Kellogg and Crystal Eastman, distress over the curtailment of civil liberties often took precedence over protesting the war itself.

But not all social workers rallied to the defense of civil liberties; nor did the AUAM remain entirely pacifistic in its reaction to events as they unfolded. Nonpacifist social workers, and a number of people who had sympathized with the peace movement in 1914 and 1915, were already moving toward an interventionist position. Leading social workers in Baltimore decried the *Survey*'s pacifism, and a large group of social work-ers in Boston wired the president to pledge support for the military defense of American rights in March 1917.[27] Rabbi Stephen Wise, a supporter of the reform-minded New Yorkers in the peace movement and other reform causes, broke with the AUAM during the same month.

By March, a radical peace faction had developed within the AUAM, which ultimately caused the desertion of founders Lillian Wald and Paul Kellogg. Norman Thomas, a Socialist, and Roger Baldwin, a St. Louis social worker, obtained positions on the AUAM board. When Eastman left temporarily to give birth to her child, Baldwin became the leader of the group. James Maurer, a leader in the Socialist Party of America, now served on AUAM's executive committee, and Scott Nearing, who lost faculty positions at two universities for his radicalism, began attending AUAM meetings. Eastman's brother Max, also a Socialist, became an active member. On the eve of the war declaration, Baldwin concentrated AUAM activities on a campaign against conscription, which resulted in the organization's fragmentation and, ultimately, dissolution.[28]

A LAST-DITCH EFFORT FOR PEACE:
THE EMERGENCY PEACE FOUNDATION

As approval of war began intruding upon some pacifists' minds, others remained unconvinced. As Gramsci and Bakhtin conceded, no hegemonic class is ever in complete control of a democratic society's ideology, culture, or language. In late February 1917, as the established groups began to waver and in some cases disband, pacifists still opposing intervention countered pro-war sentiment by giving birth to a new organization. The EPF — which included many WPP and AUAM members — worked within the democratic system of government to prevent U.S. intervention. The group's experiences served as a test of the peace movement's influence upon American foreign policy. Young newcomers to pacifism, including Louis Lochner, Rebecca Shelly, and Lella Faye Secor, along with the seasoned pacifists Balch (who belonged to the AUAM, the WPP, and the EPF) and Frederick Lynch, founded the group. Fanny Garrison Villard presided as honorary chair. Despite the large number of women leaders, the EPF's strategies to keep the United States out of the war did not utilize feminists' concerns about war, with one important and dramatic exception.[29]

The EPF emerged in a time of crisis as a last-ditch effort to stop U.S. intervention. Four goals focused the group's attention: First, the EPF demanded that the American government defer settlement of any international conflicts affecting America until the war ended. Second, the pacifists asked Congress to encourage Americans to stay out of the war zone. Third, the EPF urged action on the Moore Resolution, which provided for a congressional investigation into the charge that munitions interests virtually purchased large newspapers. Last, and most important, the EPF demanded that Congress consult the people by popular referendum before declaring war.[30]

The group appointed correspondents in congressional districts nationwide to direct the propaganda in that district and to urge constituents to wire Wilson, asking him "to keep us out of war." Activists called upon their legislators, telling them to oppose every measure designed to draw the nation into war.

The EPF linked itself with historic American figures by calling its members "peace patriots." The "peace patriots" held a mass meeting in Washington, D.C., on Lincoln's birthday; then, on Washington's birthday, they secured a hearing before the Senate Committee on Foreign Relations. College students, both men and women, warned the committee that U.S. belligerency would provoke a breach of civil liberties.[31]

The national Woman's Peace Party had voiced approval of the EPF's goals, listed above, but the EPF's opposition to armed neutrality contrasted sharply with the WPP's and the AUAM's support of that policy. Secor formulated the group's policy on the armed neutrality question. She conceived of an alternative to armed neutrality, modeling her idea on two previous concepts: University of Wisconsin professor Julia Grace Wales's neutral conference plan, and Eastman's plan to avert war with Mexico. Secor envisioned the establishment of peace commissions, made up of representatives from the United States and the belligerent nations, to work out a peace plan. The EPF held a model commission in New York from 19 to 24 March 1917.[32]

The pacifists worked most feverishly on the referendum issue. Senator La Follette and Representative George Huddleston (D-Alabama) introduced bills calling for a popular referendum on war, but both measures expired in committee. After Warren Bailey (D-Pennsylvania) introduced a new referendum bill, the EPF, in conjuction with the AUAM, mailed every voter in his or her district a postcard requesting support for the measure. Neither this effort, nor the EPF's appeal that the House and Senate Rules Committees insert a rule requiring a referendum before the United States could declare war, met with success. When the EPF could not compel Congress to pass a referendum, it urged legislators to appeal directly to the German Reichstag. The German people, they reasoned, endorsed the war because Germany needed protection against Russia; but as of March, Russia was no longer a czardom. This suggestion also proved futile.[33]

As their penultimate act, Secor, Shelly, and Balch inserted a full-page advertisement in the *New York Times* on behalf of the EPF. The ad solicited money to pay for inserts in other papers and called upon "**MOTHERS, DAUGHTERS, AND WIVES OF MEN**" to keep the United States out of war. The campaign was so effective, Balch rejoiced, that the EPF staff had to store the money it received in wastebaskets.[34]

The group's final strategy to avert war met with a governmental brick wall. On 2 April members arranged for pacifists from all over the nation to converge on Capitol Hill for a rally and parade. But at the last minute, Washington officials denied parade permits to both pacifist and patriotic groups. Congressional representatives also rebuffed the EPF's efforts to meet with them.[35]

During its final meeting on 25 July 1917, after Congress voted against the pacifists, the EPF applauded itself as the group most unflinchingly steadfast in opposing war. "Instead of working as an isolated group of intellectuals aloof from the people," the EPF "opened up a channel through which Americans might express their sentiments on war and peace . . . it offered the people an opportunity to give their emotions expression and to feel that they might have an influence upon the actions of Congress" thereby bridging the gap between "private" reflection and "public" responsibilities. The EPF applauded the expressions of antiwar sentiment that pacifists relied on in pleading with Congress to reject the war measure.[36] Yet, clearly, their fervent appeals did not alter the pro-war vote.

Indeed, the EPF inadvertently aided the Wilson administration and its congressional backers. By working within the system to avoid the declaration of war, the EPF implicitly legitimized that system and demonstrated the power of hegemonic rule. Although neither the executive nor the legislative branch even considered a referendum on the war declaration, the EPF still maintained its faith in the United States as a democratic nation.

American citizens were supposed to be sovereign and to rule themselves: however, in the instance of foreign policy in 1917, the people had little voice. Moreover, if elected officials represented the people in a democratic government, then lawmakers did not reflect their constituency very accurately in the war debate. The historians Arthur Link and David Thelen believed voters would have rejected U.S. intervention in a popular referendum, whereas Congress voted overwhelmingly for it.[37] Senator La Follette did not think Congress reflected public sentiment. He asked, "Are the people of this country being so well represented in this [debate over war] that we need to go abroad to give other people control of their governments?" Despite a preponderance of dovish public sentiment, hawkishness predominated in the legislature. The question was, why?[38]

NATIONAL HONOR AND MALE HONOR: GENDER AND THE CONGRESSIONAL DEBATE OVER WAR

Representative Meyer London (Socialist-New York) asserted that the debate over U.S. participation in the war centered on a choice between U.S.-style democratic diplomacy on the one hand, and European autocratic diplomacy on the other, which he described as "jargon . . . about national honor and dignity." As a democracy, London suggested, the United States ought to steer clear of such "jargon." But congressmen debating intervention viewed manly honor and dignity *as the cornerstone of a strong democracy* and as necessary elements in reinvigorating masculinity and strengthening American democracy to fight against European autocracy. "If we are to take part in this gigantic conflict," declared

Nicholas Longworth (R-Ohio), "we ought to take a man's part . . . [and] make war with what energy and efficiency we may." "In girding up our loins as a Nation for the serious burden cast upon us," urged Joe H. Eagle (D-Texas), "we shall need every ounce of strength of a united people." Hawkish sentiment pervaded the Capitol because war was seen as a means of reinvigorating democracy, and, concomitantly, as a weapon against autocracy.[39]

During the debate in Congress, both pro-war and antiwar congressmen spoke of upholding American rights, exporting American values to Europe, strengthening national honor and white manhood, and protecting American women and children. Congressmen arguing in favor of the resolution insisted that war would toughen the nation's manhood. But even many of those speaking *against* war conceded that while they could not vote for intervention, they nevertheless pledged energetic, patriotic support once the United States intervened. The power of nationalism, which was equated with masculinity, loomed large in President Wilson's speech, in the setting of congressional deliberations, and in the debate itself.

Given the pervasiveness of nationalism, pacifists attempting to influence legislators faced formidable barriers. Since most lawmakers' minds were made up before debate began, outsiders' attempts to influence them came too late. "I despair of success in any attempt," Charles Reavis (R-Nebraska) lamented to his colleagues on 6 April, "to influence the vote of the committee [of the House of Representatives]." Benjamin Johnson (D-Kentucky) agreed. "Every man, woman, and child in the Nation as well as those throughout the world" knew that Congress had determined to vote for war. The vote, insisted Johnson, "is a mere formality. With that situation standing out before me, I shall refrain from saying what I might have said if the die had not been cast already." Congressmen prepared their speeches beforehand, allowing little actual give-and-take or exchange of ideas between the pro and con side of the issue. Occasionally, colleagues asked permission to question a speaker, but legislators frequently rejected such interruptions. Many congressmen did not want to debate at all; they argued that "war already exists," and that therefore debate was futile. Newspaper reporters who announced well in advance of the congressional debate that "It is to be war with Germany" did much to create this illusion.[40]

President Wilson confirmed the notion that the decision for war had already been made. In his War Message, he foreshadowed many of the militaristic terms that the legislators used in their debate. "We are now about to accept the gauge of battle with this natural foe to liberty," proclaimed the president, "and shall, if necessary, spend the whole force of the Nation to check and nullify [Germany's] pretensions and its power." Wilson used the present tense in his War Message, indicating that the legislative branch could do nothing to halt the march to war, because war was, indeed, already happening. "We desire no conqest, no dominion," announced the president. "It will be all the easier for us to conduct ourselves as belligerents in a high spirit of right and fairness because we act without animus." Woodrow Wilson fully expected acceptance of the war declaration.[41]

In his speech, the president reinforced his power as commander-in-chief of the armed services and his primacy as foreign policy maker. Behind-the-scenes diplomatic maneuverings between White House officials and their counterparts in London and Berlin allowed little participation from the people's representatives.[42] By the time the president asked for a declaration of war, it was too late to alter diplomacy. As Representative Halvor Steenerson (R-Minnesota) stated, "Even though Constitutionally the Congress only has power to declare war, the President's power with regard to foreign relations is so encompassing that Congress functions merely as a rubber stamp. I regret that the representatives . . . have no choice except between repudiation of the whole administering of our foreign affairs and supporting what is proposed."[43] Thus, the legislators themselves realized that with respect to foreign policy, presidential power compromised Congress's autonomy. Such institutional constraints on lawmakers were part of the interventionists' ability to obtain support for war.

The setting of the congressional debate reinforced the traditions of seniority and precedence that restricted the opinions of legislators with less experience. Influential members of Congress spoke first, and for longer periods of time. Freshmen congressmen were not encouraged to speak at all during the debate. For example, newly elected Representative John F. Miller (R-Washington) apologized for his impertinence when he took the floor briefly, late on 6 April, to endorse the war declaration. Freshman Representative Jeannette Rankin (R-Montana), the first and only woman seated in the Sixty-fifth Congress, later regretted that she had not spoken against the resolution. Her "no" vote nevertheless became symbolic of the feminist pacifist movement.[44]

Congressmen presented their speeches for or against the war in an atmosphere of militarism that favored the pro-war side. Speakers conjured masculine, hawkish images in the military atmosphere that pervaded the chamber. President Wilson arrived at the Capitol surrounded by a cavalry of military officers who flanked him on both sides during the War

Message. During a heated exchange, Representative John L. Burnett (D-Alabama) admonished Representative Thomas Heflin (D-Alabama) for his eagerness in sending others to war but not enlisting himself. The presiding chair, Representative John J. Fitzgerald (D-New York), ordered the sergeant-at-arms to approach Burnett with the mace, a long staff used as a display of authority in the chamber. The wielding of this war relic from the Middle Ages reminded lawmakers that militarism ruled the House in scuffles between representatives (as it ruled in the outcome of the 1917 war debate).[45]

Nearly all legislators voting against the declaration, especially in the House, explained that their "no" votes reflected their antiwar constituency. One representative voting "yes" claimed his electorate wanted war. But the opinions of the people Congress served formed only part of the debate. Lawmakers commented on many issues, including America's readiness to fight, the legal issues surrounding submarine warfare, the rights of neutral nations, Americans' rights to travel during wartime, the interests of munitions makers in fomenting belligerency, the preparedness of U.S. soldiers to engage in combat, German and British atrocities committed against the United States, foreign policy procedures, and American opinion on intervention.

Representing the concerns of pacifist groups, for example, Meyer London asked for a renewed effort to call belligerents together to end the war, an idea forwarded by the AUAM, the WPP, and the EPF. Noninterventionists did not, however, identify themselves as pacifists. They articulated arguments against waging war with Germany but not against war in general. (Representative William E. Mason, Republican from Illinois, was the exception. As a Christian nation, he said, the United States should never wage war.) A few congressmen, such as Mason and Edward J. King (R-Illinois), indirectly articulated some of the feminist pacifism of the early WPP and of the women in the EPF.[46]

The bulk of the discussion centered, however, on American rights and responsibilities as a neutral nation, which legislators proffered as a measure of national strength. Among the advocates of war, Representative Byron P. Harrison (D-Mississippi) spoke of the "defense of our fundamental rights and for the preservation of the rights of humanity. . . . We enter [the war] asking nothing for ourselves save the glory that comes of fighting for the rights and liberties of mankind." In the Senate, Gilbert M. Hitchcock (D-Nebraska), another supporter of intervention, believed that Americans would fight to "maintain our independence as a great nation."[47]

On the other side, representatives used the same issue of rights to argue *against* U.S. intervention. Representative Claude Kitchin (D-North Carolina) agreed that Germany had violated the U.S. rights of neutrality, but he then recalled several other instances of violation against which the United States had chosen not to retaliate. "Why should we not forgo for the time being the violation of our rights by Germany, and do as we did with Great Britain, do as we did with Mexico, and thus save the universe from being wrapped in the flames of war?" Senator La Follette insisted similarly that, if the United States declared war against Germany for legal infractions, then Wilson would be justified in declaring war against Great Britain, as well. Representative Mason argued that submarine warfare was a new weapon in the world's arsenal and that "arbitration should determine the legal status of submarine warfare, not war."[48] Kitchin, La Follette, and Mason used their opponents' rhetoric of American rights to argue against intervention, by pointing out the fallacy of declaring war against Germany when, in similar cases involving other nations, the United States had remained at peace.

Other congressmen alluded more pointedly to strength and vigor and to fears of weakness and impotence. Representative John Charles Linthicum (D-Maryland), for example, spoke of "dedicat[ing] ourselves, our country, our manhood to the cause of freedom." Alben W. Barkley (D-Kentucky), used the term *impotence* to describe a "contemptible nation" that did not retaliate when provoked. In the Senate, Henry F. Ashurst (D-Arizona) commented, "We must present to other nations an unweakened fiber, a courage both moral and physical, a mind free from trash and slush, flexed muscles and sinews that have not been debilitated, or degenerated by sensuality, security, and luxury." Nations, like men, according to this rhetoric, must maintain through battle and conflict the strength and effi- ciency that a feminized culture of consumption had eroded. "I vote for this joint resolution to make war," echoed Senator Warren G. Harding (R-Ohio), "not a war thrust upon us, but a war declared in response to affronts. . . . a war that will at least put a soul into our American life."[49]

Femininity was also a direct target of some congressmen's speeches. Representative Augustus P. Gardner (R-Massachusetts) alluded to the protests of the WPP and other feminist pacifists but urged that "today we leave the seat of ease and we enter the arena of blood and lust, where true men are to be found. . . . Let him who wavers lag behind." King spoke gravely of the nation's manhood, which had for too long been listening to "the charming voice of the Goddess of Peace." (Curiously, despite such words, he voted *against* the resolution.) Some members portrayed females as helpless victims in need of protection. Representative Henry De La

Warr Flood (D-Virgina) opened the debate in the House with a reference to another statesman's comments on war: "'In the calamities of war children are exempted and spared on the score of their age and women from respect to their sex.'"[50] Flood established the boundary lines between an active manhood and a helpless womanhood that legislators maintained during the proceedings. The representatives justified waging war against a threat to the nation's victimized womanhood. As an added bonus, they believed war would bolster the nation's manhood, which was supposedly positioned dangerously on the brink of impotence since the nation had battled Spain in 1898.

In the minds of some legislators, keeping the reins of power in the hands of Anglo Americans was akin to maintaining a strong democracy; conversely, they assumed that a military defeat would spell a weakened white race. William Goodwin (D-Arkansas) asked, "How will it appear . . . [at the end of the war], if this Republic should be Japanized, Mexicanized, and Prussianized?" And noninterventionist Ernest Lundeen (FL-Minnesota) asked, "Shall we further bleed our own race white that the yellow peril may stand back and win in some final day of reckoning?"[51] Racist interpretations of war, used by members on both sides of the debate, thus intersected with sexist notions of weak femininity and a strong, white manhood.

Pro-war congressmen were confident the war declaration would pass overwhelmingly, and not wanting to hear discussion at all, they asked their colleagues simply to *act* against German aggression. Thoughtful hesitation, in other words, signified weakness. Representative Clarence B. Miller (R-Minnesota) demanded, "This is no time to quibble about procedure . . . it is time for united effort." In the other chamber, Senator Claude A. Swanson (D-Virginia) firmly contended that "we cannot avoid it [war]. The only wise, manly and honorable course for us to pursue is to accept the conditions of war precipitated by Germany [and] wage this war efficiently and successfully."[52] Seeing the situation as cut-and-dried, or at least presenting it as such, the pro-war side resented even the procedure of debate.

Despite frequent assertions that Americans must either defend their nation or sink back like cowards, some pro-war members admitted the war issue was in fact complex. Representative William J. Fields (D-Kentucky), for example, spoke of the difficulties of feeling one way and being compelled by duty to act another way: "I can't let my personal feelings come between me and my duty to my country." Wisconsin's Democratic senator Paul O. Husting said that he intended to support the war declaration. Nevertheless, he added sadly, "I wish that the crisis which now confronts us was such that I might find it compatible with what I conceive to be my duty as a Senator. . . . But our desires are often incompatible with our plain duty, and that is the solemn situation I find myself in to-day." Legislators chafed at voting for a war that would send innocent people to death. But interventionists generally discarded equivocation as effeminate weakness. Senator William Alden Smith (R-Michigan) worried, "I do not want it said of me that . . . I was found wanting in the hour of need to sustain the freedom of our institutions." Barkley charged that lack of unified support for the war rendered the United States "impotent and contemptible." He asked his colleagues to imagine what history would be like if the United States had shunned war in 1812 and 1898.[53]

Congressmen who *wanted* to vote for peace but who nevertheless felt it their duty to vote for war produced empty speeches all too often on the antiwar side. Many noninterventionists merely followed the lead of the pro-war side rather than speaking out against war. For example, instead of talking about the United States' heroic pacifists of the past, noninterventionist congressmen succumbed to glorified images of war used repeatedly by the interventionist faction.

Representative Frederick A. Britten (R-Illinois) hearkened back to the Revolutionary War, as did many of his pro-war colleagues. He recalled Valley Forge, where a German general had helped the men to survive; in effect, Britten used an image of war to combat war. Similarly, Senator James K. Vardaman (D-Mississippi) stated: "It ought to be a highly prized opportunity in the hour of trial . . . for a citizen of the Republic to offer his service in defense of his flag."[54] His point, that Germany was not solely responsible for war crimes, was lost in his glorified images of war. Speeches like these did the noninterventionist side little good.

Britten could not explain why he and his noninterventionist colleagues were helpless to stop the forces of war. Yet neither could he explain prowar sentiment. "There is something in the air . . . stronger than you or I can resist . . . [the force] is picking us up bodily and literally forcing us to vote for this resolution when down deep in our hearts we are as opposed to it as people back home."[55]

But some noninterventionist congressmen, including George Norris, did not flounder. With statements similar to those made by the AUAM and the EPF, Norris blasted the newspapers' manufactured war sentiment. After reading a letter from a member of the New York Stock Exchange on how much profit war could bring the United States, he asked his colleagues: "To whom does war bring prosperity" — those who will lose their lives in Europe or those encouraging war?[56] Norris stated with precision that those who stood to gain financially were responsible for creating a pro-war sentiment.

The voice of opposition in Congress began to dwindle as the debate continued into the early morning hours of 6 April. As time ran out, the noninterventionists began their speeches by admitting defeat and then laced their remarks with promises to support the war effort. "This resolution will pass," acknowledged Representative William L. Igoe (D-Missouri). "When it does I know there will no longer be any division of sentiment." In the Senate, William J. Stone and Vardaman voted against the resolution, but each man promised to give the president soldiers and money to fight the war. Representative Johnson said, "If any hope whatever for peace were left, I might argue, plead and pray for peace." Voting against the resolution, Representative Harry E. Hull (R-Iowa) hoped that if the measure passed, "God [would] grant that we fight with all our might." Representative Charles H. Sloan (R-Nebraska) began his plea for nonintervention by boasting of his state's service record, "a record unequalled by any state." In the Senate, even Norris began his speech by offering to wave the flag if the vote was cast for war. One representative, Charles H. Dillon (R-South Dakota), nevertheless remained stalwart even at this late hour. "We stand on the brink of war, but it has not yet been declared," he said. "The door is still open; let us not close it." Yet most noninterventionists — ironically after they had pointed to a lack of popular support for war — succumbed to the very pro-war sentiment they claimed their constituents did not possess, using phrases such as "fighting with all our might" and "moving swiftly to victory."[57] When the secretary read the last roll call, the House voted 373 to 50 for war; the Senate voted 82 to 6.

Although the vote went against them, the EPF pacifists had at least increased public participation in the debate. Some constituents who wrote to their representatives in Congress referred to the EPF's advertisement, which urged people to contact legislators. The letters printed in the *Congressional Record* showed an electorate not won over by simple homilies; indeed, a wide variety of opinions existed on a very complex subject. Neither did antiwar representatives present fatuous arguments. But clearly they felt an enormous pressure to "vote a man's vote," as Rankin's brother advised her to do before she disappointed him. As Illinois Republican James R. Mann asked fearfully in the House, "What position will we be in if we were to declare to the world that we are afraid to go to war?"[58]

THE AFTERMATH OF THE WAR DECLARATION

The EPF evolved into the People's Council of America for Peace and Democracy after the congressional vote, an organization which continued radical protest by calling for the protection of civil liberties, the taxation of war profits, and the maintenance of labor standards during wartime. Both the WPP and the AUAM backed off considerably from their stand in opposition to the government.

The WPP national board's policy statement of 25 October 1917 defended the kind of patriotic rhetoric used by the Massachusetts branch. Still concerned with being seen as "legitimate," the national board maintained its support of the principles of international statesmanship and a police force "to which an ever-increasing number of publicists and government officials are now giving their assent." The women boasted that *their* contention — "that all future progress of the race waits upon the abolition of war" — had become the "accepted and publicly expressed belief alike of leaders of the war parties and of the various 'pacifist' groups, who are all determined that this shall be the last great war." WPP leaders blurred the differences between pro-war and antiwar factions, in effect making peace obtainable only through a united war effort in which the WPP claimed a role. Carefully falling short of connecting Wilson with actual battle, the women instead applauded his "wise mastery of political problems," which they believed would result in the abolition of war. All this, they claimed, stood as proof that the WPP "is not only a loyal body devoted to the welfare of our country, but has a certain leadership" in demanding a course of peace. The WPP remained a reputable organization by never asking for an "immediate peace" or demanding "peace at any price." Mentioning women only twice (once, in calling for citizenship for women of all nations, and again, in expressing sympathy to the women of belligerent nations),[59] the WPP's rhetoric after U.S. intervention documented the effacement of the feminist pacifist identity its members had constructed in 1915, and which they had replaced with a patriotic wartime citizen, poised to take on the democratic privileges of suffrage.

Finally, the leaders assured the government that the WPP had thrown "no verbal brick-bats" in retaliation at those critical of "'pacifist'" groups, which by this time included many newspapers and interventionist congressmen. Significantly, the women placed the word *pacifist* in quotation marks, indicating that they, like their detractors, had become suspicious of the term.

Examples of negative attitudes toward the word *pacifist* on the eve of intervention abound. The *New York Times* printed an article about the New

York City Board of Education trying to oust pacifist teachers in its districts. The same edition featured a piece about the American League of California, which denounced the EPF advertisement (calling on mothers, daughters, and wives to reject war). The article noted that clubwomen "have added their voice to that of the nation's manhood, aligning themselves with the East in support of the determination to uphold the country's honor and the world cause of humanity." The *Times* also quoted the Women's Preparedness Committee. In this case, the women equated pacifism with weakness, and patriotism with female strength: "The hysterical cry of the feminine pacifist to arouse the timidity in American women is an insult to our sex, and is deserving of the sternest rebuke by the patriotic womanhood of our country and must be repudiated." The Women's Anti-Suffrage Associaton placed an even more telling ad in the *Times* in which they stated that men should reject woman suffrage "because the world war has shown that a Democracy must be strong to be safe. Many suffrage leaders are Pacifists. Every element now working to weaken our Government, *Pacifist, Socialist, Feminist*, favors Woman Suffrage. Woman Suffrage will weaken the Government." The war, according to these women, proved that democracy must be male to be strong.[60]

The WPP split over the issue of whether pacifists should perform war-relief work. Because journalists predicted war well in advance of the actual declaration, the WPP already faced the issue months before official intervention. On 22 February the national board of the WPP wrote a letter to Carrie Chapman Catt (WPP co-founder and leader of the National American Woman Suffrage Association), asking her not to volunteer women for war-relief work. Catt proceeded to do exactly the opposite. As a result, antagonism developed between the women of the WPP and their co-founder. Nevertheless, many WPP women soon changed their minds about war work. Jane Addams became involved with Herbert Hoover's Department of Food Administration, and Lucia Ames Mead encouraged state WPP chairmen to "enter on some form of public service and thus let our opponents perceive our readiness to serve our country." Catt, and other suffragists, hoped that war service would increase women's chances of gaining the vote.[61]

Initially critical of the U.S. government, the founders of the AUAM toned down their rhetoric appreciably after the congressional vote. The more the group continued its opposition to U.S. policy, the more uncomfortable some members became. "We cannot plan continuance of our program which entails friendly governmental relations," warned William Wald, "and at the same time drift into being a party of opposition to the government."[62] Like the national WPP, Wald wanted to maintain access to government leaders. Eastman saw the AUAM as shaping presidential politics, and keeping Wilson "in touch with liberal anti-militarist sentiment," by working *with* and not against the government. Eastman conflated the government's and AUAM's hopes, agreeing with Kellogg that the AUAM should "enlist the rank and file of the people, who make for progressivism the country over, in a movement for a civil solution of this world-wide conflict and fire them with a vision of the beginnings of a U.S. of the World."[63] Kellogg and Eastman approved the president's vision of the Americanization of the war, an ideal that established a clear connection between progressivism and Americanization.

The probing questions the AUAM asked before the declaration of war disappeared, replaced by a more conciliatory attitude toward the U.S. government. Defending its members as progressive pacifists, the AUAM disapproved of the declaration of war but still upheld the United States as having a superior form of democratic government: "America was stronger to bring the nations into a lasting federation for peace." Furthermore, members pledged noninterference with the prosecution of the war on the grounds that they must not obstruct "our own government in its prosecution of a war upon which the nation through the act of its elected representatives (elected to be sure upon a basis of very incompatible democracy) has embarked." Although they accepted the United States as a democracy, they opposed "the general abrogation of civil liberty, which [is] manifestly not essential to the prosecution of the war, and which in a war such as this, avowedly fought for the sake of democracy, [is] inappropriate."[64]

Radicals such as Norman Thomas, however, saw problems more far-reaching than the government's failure to respond to pacifists' desires. "The situation is at once so confused and interwoven," wrote Thomas to Eastman, "that one cannot take hold of any aspect of the problem without finding himself dealing with the whole question of the wrong organization of society; capitalistic exploitation, militarism, contempt of civil liberties . . . these are all aspects of the wrong basis of our social life."[65] The New York City Woman's Peace Party would add "patriarchy" and "sexism" to Thomas's list. Their pacifism, infused with their feminist perspective, sustained the New York women through the war declaration and beyond.

NOTES

1. Charles DeBenedetti, *Origins of the Modern American Peace Movement, 1915–1929* (Millwood, N.Y.: KTO Press, 1978), 82.

2. John Whiteclay Chambers II, ed., *The Eagle and the Dove: The American Peace Movement and U.S. Foreign Policy, 1900–1922*, 2nd ed. (Syracuse, N.Y.: Syracuse University Press, 1991), xlv. I have limited this study to progressive pacifists, excluding socialists and ethnic Americans — especially German and Irish Americans — who were also very much a part of continued resistance to war. The New York City WPP will be treated extensively in chapter 5.

3. John A. Thompson, *Reformers and War: American Progressive Publicists and the First World War* (Cambridge: Cambridge University Press, 1987), 168.

4. Paul U. Kellogg, "The Fighting Issues," *Survey*, 17 February 1917, 573–574; Jordan quoted in *The American Peace Movement and Social Reform, 1898–1918*, by C. Roland Marchand (Princeton, N.J.: Princeton University Press, 1972), 250–251.

5. Pinchot quoted in *Reformers*, by Thompson, 151.

6. "A War Program for Liberals," *New Republic*, 31 March 1917, 249–250.

7. Hamilton Holt, "The Crisis," *Independent*, 12 March 1917, 434.

8. *New Republic*, 14 April 1917, 307.

9. Thompson, *Reformers*, 161.

10. Quoted in *Reformers*, by Thomspon, 169.

11. Ibid., 175.

12. Warren F. Kuehl, *Hamilton Holt: Journalist, Internationalist, Educator* (Gainesville: University of Florida Press, 1960), 116; Edward Devine, "Ourselves and Europe: I," *Survey*, 4 November 1916, 100.

13. Michael A. Lutzker, "The Pacifist as Militarist: A Critique of the American Peace Movement, 1898–1914," *Societas* 5 (Spring 1975): 103.

14. Barbara J. Steinson, *American Women's Activism in World War I* (New York: Garland Press, 1982), 234.

15. Arthur S. Link, *Wilson: Campaigns for Peace and Progressivism, 1916–1917* (Princeton, N.J.: Princeton University Press, 1965), 252, 255.

16. Wilson's speech appeared in the *Independent*, 5 February 1917, 224–227.

17. Carleton J. Hayes, "Which? War Without a Purpose? Or Armed Neutrality with a Purpose?" *Survey*, 10 February 1917, 535–538. For a discussion of how peace workers influenced Wilson's foreign policy decision, see Chambers, *Eagle and the Dove*, liv–lv.

18. James Parker Martin, "The American Peace Movement and the Progressive Era, 1910–1917," (Ph.D. diss., Rice University, 1975), 71. The AUAM and the WPP also praised Wilson's speech.

19. "If We Must Enter War," *Independent*, 19 February 1917, 289.

20. Marchand, *American Peace Movement*, 157.

21. "Statement, Issued by Five Members of the Executive Board, Massachusetts Branch of the Woman's Peace Party," n.d., SR 12.5, Box 6, WPP Papers, SCPC.

22.   Ibid.

23.   "Statement Formulated by a Conference of Members of the Executive Board and Representatives of Affiliated and Local Branches of the WPP," 21 February 1917, SR 12.2, WPP Papers, SCPC.

24.   "Memoranda on Purposes of War," (n.d.), reel 10.1, AUAM Papers, SCPC.

25.   Kellogg, "Fighting Issues," 572, 574, 577.

26.   Ibid., 577.

27.   *Survey*, 24 March 1917, 729–730.

28.   See Marchand, *American Peace Movement*, for the mutations in AUAM membership during this period, 252–253.

29.   Chambers, *Eagle and the Dove*, in his introductory essay, deals with the pacifists' attempts at changing foreign policy in 1917. Lochner, Shelly, and Secor came to the EPF from their experiences on the Ford Peace Ship, an ill-fated attempt in 1915 to schedule peace meetings in neutral European countries. See Barbara S. Kraft, *The Peace Ship: Henry Ford's Pacifist Adventure in the First World War* (New York: Macmillan, 1978). This New York-based Emergency Peace Federation was distinct from the Chicago EPF, formed in 1914. See Marchand, *American Peace Movement*, 148–149, and 249–250; also Merle Curti, *Peace or War: The American Struggle, 1636–1936* (New York: W.W. Norton, 1936), 249–257.

30.   "The Emergency Peace Federation" flyer, (n.d.) misc. box, CDGA, EPF Papers, SCPC; miscellaneous minutes, (n.d.) misc. box, CDGA, EPF Papers, SCPC.

31.   "Emergency Peace Federation" flyer.

32.   *New York Times*, 22 March 1917; see also "Emergency Peace vs. War Emergency," *Survey*, 31 March 1917, 762.

33.   Miscellaneous minutes, CDGA, EPF Papers, SCPC. For a history of the war referendum in American politics, see Ernest C. Bolt, Jr., *Ballots Before Bullets: The War Referendum Approach to Peace in America, 1914–1941* (Charlottesville: University Press of Virginia, 1977).

34.   *New York Times*, 29 March 1917, 5; Steinson, *American Women's Activism*, 247.

35.   Steinson, *American Women's Activism*, 247–248.

36.   "Miscellaneous Minutes: Executive council's statement at last meeting" (n.d.), misc. box, CDGA EPF Papers, SCPC.

37.   Link, *Wilson: Campaigns*, 429 n. 103; Link, *Woodrow Wilson: Revolution, War and Peace*, (Arlington Heights, Ill.: Harlan Davidson, 1979), 22; David P. Thelen, *Robert M. La Follette and the Insurgent Spirit* (Boston: Little, Brown and Co., 1976), 131–132.

38.   *Congressional Record*, 65th Congress, 1917, 228; T. J. Jackson Lears posed the same question in "The Concept of Cultural Hegemony: Problems and Possibilities," *American Historical Review*, 90 (June 1985): 586.

39.   *Congressional Record*, 330, 396, 358.

40. Ibid., 356, 370–371, 201; *New York Times*, 31 March 1917, 1.

41. Ibid., 120.

42. With the exceptions of important pro-war Congressmen Swanson, Knox, and Flood, who had already met with Wilson. See Link, *Wilson: Campaigns*, 422–423.

43. *Congressional Record*, 404; Rep. Edward Keating (D-Colorado) voted against the resolution because he feared Congress would continue to lose power to the president and secretaries of army and navy if the declaration passed, ibid., 348.

44. Ibid., 408; see Kevin S. Giles, *Flight of the Dove: The Story of Jeannette Rankin* (Beaverton, Ore.: Lochsa Experience Press, 1980), 89–94.

45. *Congressional Record*, 373.

46. Ibid., 330, 328. Women's antiwar opinions were mentioned, but feminist pacifism, that is, pacifism based on women as political participants, was not given as a reason for staying out of war. Representative Burnett indicated that he thought women would be more likely to vote against war. "In the West where women vote, 1,000 wives, mothers and sisters voted for Wilson's peace, even though the Republican candidate offered suffrage," ibid., 373.

47. *Congressional Record*, 316, 201.

48. Ibid., 333, 227, 327.

49. Ibid., 324, 375, 221, 254.

50. Ibid., 379, 342, 308.

51. Ibid., 332, 364.

52. Ibid., 328, 207.

53. Ibid., 322, 249, 391, 375.

54. Ibid., 317, 209.

55. Ibid., 317. Britten began his speech by assuring his colleagues that he was not a pacifist.

56. Ibid., 213–214.

57. Ibid., 323, 371, 342, 351, 213, 403.

58. Giles, *Flight of the Dove*, 90; *Congressional Record*, 377.

59. See Steinson, *American Women's Activism*, for the transformation of the EPF into the People's Council, modeled after the Council of the Workmen's and Soldier's Delegates in Russia, pp. 265–278. "Statement of the Executive Board of the National WPP," 25 October 1917, SR 12.2, WPP Papers, SCPC.

60. *New York Times*, 31 March 1917, 9; *New York Times* 1 April 1917, 1; *New York Times*, 1 April 1917, 2; *New York Times*, 5 November 1917, 11.

61. National Board WPP to CCC, 22 February 1917, SR 12.2, WPP Papers, SCPC; Mead to State Chairmen, 6 April 1917, SR 12.2, WPP Papers, SCPC; Neil Wynn, *From Progressivism to Prosperity: World War I and American Society* (New York: Holmes and Meier, 1986), 136.

62. Lillian Wald quoted by Crystal Eastman to Emily G. Balch, 14 June 1917, reel 10.1, AUAM Papers, SCPC.

63. Paul Kellogg quoted by Crystal Eastman to Emily Greene Balch, 14 June 1917, reel 10.1, AUAM Papers, SCPC.

64. "AUAM Wartime Program," 1 June 1917, reel 10.1, AUAM Papers, SCPC.

65. Quoted in *American Peace Movement*, by Marchand, 263–264.

5

"Women's Ways in War": The Feminist Pacifism of the New York City Woman's Peace Party

The New York City branch of the Woman's Peace Party (NYC-WPP) formulated a feminist pacifist ideology that in some ways departed from that of its parent organization. Unlike the national WPP or any other pacifist organization, the New Yorkers explored the connected oppressions of gender, class, and race in American society in their journal, *Four Lights*. As progressives began arguing for war on the basis of masculine comraderie and a reinvigorated culture and society, the national WPP's rhetoric lost intensity; the organization also "fell in" behind intervention as a means of strengthening American democracy. Pacifist rhetoric based on women's exclusive roles as nonviolent nurturers — the mother-half of humanity — lost relevancy as interventionists began persuading Americans that their democracy needed fortification through male military combat. But the New York City WPP's pacifism, based on a plurality of oppressions in American society, could not easily be absorbed — or dismissed — by interventionists' arguments.

The NYC-WPP stood in even starker contrast to the Massachusetts branch of the WPP. Whereas the New England women reinforced traditional Victorian gender roles by rejecting woman suffrage, the New Yorkers challenged those roles by disconnecting women from their conventional duties as men's helpmeets. After intervention, the Massachusetts women joined the war effort by knitting socks for U.S. soldiers, while the NYC-WPP saw war-relief work as heinous as combat itself. Furthermore, the Massachusetts branch willingly succumbed to the curtailment of citizens' rights during war. But when the New York WPP faced charges of treason for their pacifist beliefs, they continued to defend freedom of expression during war.

In criticizing wartime policies, the New York feminists also undermined the broad support President Wilson enjoyed among progressives, including most WPP members, for U.S. intervention in the Great War. Shaken by charges of treason, however, many New Yorkers backed off from active opposition during hostilities. But after the belligerent nations signed the peace treaty, the NYC-WPP's goals shifted once again.

PERSPECTIVES OF HISTORIANS OF WOMEN ON THE PROGRESSIVE ERA

Women within the national WPP and its New York City branch were all seasoned progressive reformers. The women's historian Nancy S. Dye suggested that by interpreting progressivism from a woman's perspective, historians can begin to understand the reform movement as grounded in the redefinition of relationships between home and community and between the public and private spheres of conventional Victorian social norms. Following up on Dye's suggestion, Ellen Carol Dubois analyzed how progressive women conceived of their roles in society. She maintained that a generational and ideological distinction existed among progressive women born in the 1860s and those born in the 1870s and 1880s, a difference defined by how far women were willing to go in challenging traditional standards. Earlier female reformers modeled themselves as idealized mothers and homemakers, whereas the later generation took the female worker as its ideal woman. For progressive women who came of age around 1900, paid labor, not voluntary work, became the prototype. Dubois contended that all women reformers sought to redefine public and private spaces, but that they formulated different discourses to help them make sense of their place in a male-dominated world.[1]

Barbara Sicherman is another women's historian interested in how language reflects and creates power structures in society. She expanded progressive revisionism in her analysis of female discourses within the male-dominated progressive class. "To the degree [progressive women] were dispersed into a male world," Sicherman wrote, "they felt marginal and impotent. By contrast, insofar as they defined their own agenda and created institutions that gave them authority," women felt empowered. The "language of gender," according to Sicherman, provided a way to order the world that was "useful and exhilarating."[2]

But neither Dubois nor Sicherman explored progressive women's peace activism in their works. Within the women's peace movement, older and younger women not only formulated different discourses, but they also pursued different goals. For example, in 1915 the national WPP urged that "women be given a share in deciding between war and peace in all the courts of high debate — within the home, the school, the church, the industrial order and the state." Although the U.S. government did not cooperate with the women (neither President Wilson nor the U.S. Congress consulted the WPP on the question of intervention), the national WPP nevertheless ultimately accepted the war declaration and ceased to criticize the manner in which the government decided to intervene. In other words, the organization capitulated to male authority (at least rhetorically), backing down from its demand that women be included in matters of public policy-making decisions.

The New York City WPP, by contrast, sought to change the male-dominated society and government that voted for war. While they placed hope in woman suffrage, the NYC-WPP looked for deeper solutions to a wider range of problems they saw in American society. Moreover, the NYC-WPP diverged from its parent organization in its actions, or, more accurately, in what it chose *not* to do. While most WPP women engaged in some kind of voluntary war work, the NYC-WPP refrained from such activity because they were convinced that it only exacerbated the military's presence within American society.

In its platform, the national WPP utilized a language of gender, which the NYC-WPP continued. But many of the female pacifists within the national WPP welcomed the opportunity to become involved in war work — to experience *the* national event — to help their country win the Great War. Rather than leaving women marginalized or impotent, joining the war effort — becoming "dispersed into a male world" — actually empowered them. And, to some extent, pro-war progressives encouraged women's involvement in war-relief work, making them feel welcome and needed in a male world. Offering women, and women pacifists, a role in the war effort — both paid and voluntary — became an important method used by interventionists to obtain women's consent to war.[3]

U.S. intervention in World War I and the pending woman suffrage amendment (the House passed the amendment eight months after the country declared war) formed a crossroads between feminist pacifist discourse and the experience of joining a national crusade, dominated by men, for the sake of winning votes for women.[4] The nebulous position women held in society at this historical moment ruptured the unity of goals that Dubois detected among the first and second generations of women reformers, and the unified, empowering discourse Sicherman discerned among progressive women who established their own institutions, apart from men.

A PORTRAIT OF THE NYC-WPP'S
FOUR LIGHTS EDITORS

The NYC-WPP was made up of a radical contingent of seasoned female reformers. Many of the members socialized within a literary and feminist club called Hetcrodoxy located in Greenwich Village. Pacifist members of Heterodoxy joined the NYC-WPP, using their talents as writers in the production of the group's bi-weekly journal, *Four Lights*.

Most of the editors and writers of *Four Lights* were younger progressive women, born in the 1870s and 1880s. (In 1917 the youngest editor, Freda Kirchwey, was twenty-four, and Mary White Ovington was the eldest at fifty-two.) As Dubois suggested, these younger women took the educated working woman as their model, rather than the idealized Victorian wife and mother. Katherine Anthony, Jessie Wallace Hughan, Edna Kenton, Sarah N. Cleghorn, Zoë Beckley, Margaret Lane, Madeline Z. Doty, Crystal Eastman, Tracy Mygatt, Frances Witherspoon, and Ovington were all published writers and editors. Hughan taught high school, Lou Rogers drew cartoons, Emily Greene Balch taught sociology at Wellesley, and Eastman practiced law. Eastman, Ovington, Hughan, and Kirchwey were socialists; Ovington was also a social worker, interested particularly in racial discrimination. Kirchwey, Eastman, Mygatt, and Witherspoon were active in labor issues and organizations. All of these women had attended colleges or universities. Eastman, Balch, and Hughan had degrees beyond the bachelor's. Eastman, Doty, Kirchwey, Anne Herendeen, Lane, and Rogers were married; the others remained single. Mary Ware Dennett divorced her husband. Katherine Anthony and Elisabeth Irwin, and Mygatt and Witherspoon were lesbian couples. Eastman, Doty, Anthony, Beckley, Herendeen, Irwin, Lane, Marjorie Benton Cooke, Kenton, and Fola La Follette were Heterodoxy members.

In July and August 1917, when the U.S. Justice Department investigated the NYC-WPP for alleged espionage, the women published their ancestry in *Four Lights*. Half of the twenty-eight members were eligible for membership in the Daughters of the American Revolution. But although most had been born into established New York Anglo American families (Mygatt and Witherspoon were wealthy enough to live frugally on their inheritances), they were relatively free from class allegiances. After they printed their genealogies in the 28 July 1917 issue, they begged the pardon of their readers, admitting that "we have been most provincial in our choice of a crew [of editors]. Instead of drawing from the 4 winds of the Earth we have lazily accepted the assistance of a few Mayflower descendants." Henceforth, the women promised, they would open their paper to "any race under the sun, black, white and yellow."[5]

THE STRATEGIES AND METHODS
USED BY THE NYC-WPP

The NYC-WPP created and expressed its gender-conscious views toward the war in the pages of *Four Lights*. Although the group continued the national WPP's rhetoric, the New Yorkers' strategy differed from that of the parent organization. The NYC-WPP members did not attempt to build a coalition between suffragists and antisuffragists, whose views of women's more submissive role in politics diverged from their own. The women concentrated their energies on defining and representing feminism and pacifism, perspectives they believed were inherently linked, whereas some women in the national organization, particularly those from the Massachusetts branch, thought feminism and pacifism were incompatible.

In some respects, the goals of the New York women complemented those of other pacifist groups, such as the American Union Against Militarism, the Emergency Peace Federation, and the national WPP. The NYC-WPP supported a federation of nations after the war ended, and the guarding of civil liberties against militarism. Members of the World Peace Foundation, the AUAM, and the national WPP all sought peace through the world coalition-building process of internationalism. These goals represented general reform impulses common to all progressive pacifists. Furthermore, like other progressive pacifists, the New Yorkers worked with labor and political reforms. But the NYC-WPP's journal offered fresh interpretations of the news surrounding the war and presented its readers with an alternative perspective on progressive reforms. Considering how much the NYC-WPP held in common with many other progressives, reformers may have been surprised that the content of *Four Lights* differed so markedly from that of other pacifist publications. The difference lay in the women's gendered view of American society and culture and, in particular, on the issues surrounding the war. Many *Four Lights* issues featured women's experiences and attitudes toward the war and their active opposition to U.S. intervention.

But the women's journal, and the feminist pacifism it expressed, altered as the events surrounding the war unfolded. From January 1917 until U.S. intervention in April, the women expressed the ideal of American superiority. "May America be true to her destiny, that she may keep forever her place in the sun, the hope of the world."[6] Other editors spoke approvingly of President Wilson and upheld American democracy. But when Congress voted for war in April, the NYC-WPP ceased to support the Wilson administration in its magazine and continued its radical feminist interpretations of events, imbuing news about the war with feminist meanings. When the U.S. Postal Service censored the journal in July 1917, the organization began to rethink its radical stance. In June 1918, as President Wilson began preparing for peace, the New Yorkers stopped emphasizing war and began focusing on the peace settlement. Finally, after the Paris peace conference ended and Woodrow Wilson came home to convince Americans of the virtues of the peace treaty and the League of Nations, the women shifted gears to a more radical position.

FORM AND FUNCTION OF *FOUR LIGHTS*

The publication policies of *Four Lights* differed from those of two other progressive journals representing pacifist groups, the *Independent* and the *Survey*. *Four Lights* rotated its editorial staff every week, allowing different styles and views within its pages. (It borrowed from the *Survey* the method of placing divergent opinions side by side, however.) Not simply a matter of sharing work, the practice of alternating staff became part of the women's strategy. For example, the 27 January 1917 editors, Herendeen, Kenton, and Beckley, began their issue with this note: "'*Four Lights*' will not give any of its lustre to the jewel of consistency. Each fortnightly issue will express the internationalist hope of a new Board of three volunteer editors. . . . If you do not like this number, be sure to get the next!"[7] The title of the publication derived from a poem about Magellan ("First Voyage 'Round the World"). To the right of the logo was a drawing of a sixteenth-century ship navigating choppy waters. Beneath the masthead were the words, "An Adventure in Internationalism." Reading *Four Lights* was, indeed, an adventure — an encounter with alternative views on war, peace, and American culture and society.

Herendeen, Kenton, and Beckley announced the NYC-WPP's goals and purposes — "To voice the young, uncompromising women's peace movement" — in the first issue of *Four Lights*. "Our daring and immediate aims are to 1) stop the war in Europe; 2) to federate the nations after war; 3) to guard democracy from militarism."[8] The final two aims were not, by themselves, particularly revolutionary. To call for immediate cessation of the war after the United States became embroiled in the conflict *was* radical, however.

The NYC-WPP targeted the mainstream press's views of the war as part of its goals. The women announced that they were "sending *Four Lights* free to a large list of newspapers throughout the country in the hope of sounding the new note of internationalism in the American Press."[9] *Four Lights* covered themes such as internationalism, militarism in the United States, the concerns of women during wartime, a class-based critique of U.S. involvement in the war, and negative views of progressivism and progressive discourse, topics the editors believed were absent from other newspapers.

Four Lights functioned as an alternative press by acting as a sort of clipping service, offering its readers news stories from the papers of foreign countries. For example, the 6 February 1917 issue reprinted a story from a Berlin paper, which reported a mass meeting in Vienna, where women adopted a resolution urging the men and women of the hostile countries to "'tell the world that they, too, want peace.'" Editors Tracy Mygatt, Miriam Teichner, and Mary Johnston reprinted a telegram from a European war correspondent, W. G. Shepherd, to Amos Pinchot. Shepherd seized every opportunity to ask army officers whether the people of Europe would have voted for a war. The invariable response was, "of course not." These kinds of stories, according to *Four Lights* editors, were not available to mainstream press readers.[10] Unlike the conventional press, of course, the editors of *Four Lights* made no pretense at "objective" news reporting. They recognized, however, that the major newspapers were not objective when they printed only pro-American, pro-Ally, or pro-war stories.

Four Lights editors adopted various strategies to illustrate their opposition to the war. One was to reprint news items from the daily press and then to top the story with a mocking headline. Editors Joy Young and Herendeen reprinted a news item about the Red Cross: "'The American Red Cross is the big brother of the army and the navy.'" The women topped this snippet in bold letters, "**WE THOUGHT IT WAS A GIRL.**" Young's and Herendeen's sense of irony undoubtedly came from their reading of numerous Red Cross recruitment and propaganda posters, which featured women nurses eagerly volunteering to join the war effort (see Figure 5.1). By speaking of the organization in male terms, the daily paper overlooked female domination of the Red Cross. *Four Lights'* title suggested that women's work went unrealized by the press and that the Red Cross recruitment posters fooled women into expecting recognition for their work.[11]

Another strategy was to juxtapose two conflicting opinions on the same page. For example, the 2 June 1917 issue offered a number of fragments

FIGURE 5.1

Source: *I Summon You to Comradeship in the Red Cross*, World War I Red Cross Poster, C. 1918, Harrison Fisher, artist. Gift of John W. Campbell to the Museum of the City of New York.

the editors reprinted alongside each other. Below the headline, "Little Words of Love" (also a mocking title), the editors printed a comment, "'There is no hate in our hearts for the German people,'" made by President Wilson. The editors then described a number of German workers whose U.S. employers had discharged them because of their ethnicity. The next item, under the title, "Still More War Horrors," described Lord Beresford's reaction at London's Savoy Hotel when he discovered he had been eating off plates made in Germany. He and a number of guests hurled their dinnerware to the floor. By placing the stories one right after the other, the editors revealed two different expressions of hatred toward Germans. In the first case, prejudice caused unemployment and hardship for Germans living in the United States. In the second, animosity toward Germans resulted in a ridiculous display of childishness, as grown men and women enjoyed a fine meal and then rioted when they discovered the origin of the plates. Reading the stories sequentially made readers aware of the different ways in which hatred manifested itself during the war.[12]

AN ALTERNATIVE INTERPRETATION OF PROGRESSIVE INTERNATIONALISM

The New York women also differed from other progressive pacifists in their definition of internationalism. The feminists' gender-conscious analyses of culture and society led them to conceive of internationalism as a truly equitable relationship among nations. As women's rights advocates, the NYC-WPP understood male domination as the root of female subjugation. They transferred the model of domination-subjugation to their assessment of world politics. Powerful nations such as the United States, according to the NYC-WPP, unjustly mastered smaller countries. As the women rejected male domination of women, so they rejected U.S. domination of other countries.

In the first issue of *Four Lights*, Kenton charged that arbitrary political boundaries inflamed nationalist passions, which then led to war. She described a mythical two-dimensional land called Flatland, a thinly disguised euphemism for the United States. Kenton detailed this two-dimensional space as an "effectual prison" made up of imaginary lines in which dwelled a spiritually flat people. The United States conceived of the lines *within* its geography as highly imaginary; each state traded with the other under generous terms. But when the country looked north, south, east, or west, it became "Flatlanderishly" intent upon making larger group development and exchange as bitterly difficult as possible. Although U.S. diplomats' nationalistic policies were bound by geography, the citizenry included "fast increasing numbers of [internationalists]," who watched sorrowfully as the nationalists defended their nation's boundaries in the World War by killing innocent people. Kenton claimed that internationalists wanted to rid the world of political boundaries and prevent war by doing so.[13]

Others suggested forming a "U.S. Relations Commission" to promote goodwill among nations. The U.S. War Department planned for hostilities between nations it regarded as potential enemies, charged Margaret Lane and Martha Gruening. A Relations Commission would formulate plans for maintaining peace. The practice of suggesting solutions became part of *Four Lights'* formula: the editors did not stop at criticizing their government (the war department fomented hostilities in peacetime) but went on to suggest ways to correct wrongs (instituting a Relations Commission).[14]

The editors recognized the dangers in over-zealous nationalism. They highlighted a series of thought-provoking queries related to internationalism, nationalism, and militarism. One piece quoted the Frenchman Ernest Lavisse, who yearned for a day when "all the nations would put their banners together and, after having saluted the revered symbols for the last time, burn them in a joy fire." The editors responded by asking, "Why not?"[15]

To promote an awareness of how nations were related to one another, editors Mary Ware Dennett and Mary Knickerbocker Angell printed what they called "The ABC of Internationalism," an alphabetical listing of the Library of Congress's catalogue of international organizations under the first three letters of the alphabet. If the mainstream press's conception of international relations provoked antagonism during wartime (as other peace organizations charged), then the NYC-WPP offered proof that cooperation and goodwill between nations existed in the form of a multitude of international organizations.

Dennett and Angell also utilized the strategy of placing contradictory opinions side by side to achieve a symbolic dialogue between internationalists and nationalists. On the 10 March 1917 issue's back page, the editors featured "Preparing for Peace," a piece about the American Federation of Labor's attempts to resist militarism by organizing a pan-American federation. The adjacent article, titled "Preparing for War," told a story about the Idaho legislature's consideration of an alien land law, which constituted discrimination against Japanese workers. Juxtaposing the articles encouraged readers to consider both the nationalist and internationalist viewpoints together; the comparison would convince readers that the nationalist viewpoint fostered war.[16]

Four Lights writers challenged the unquestioning certainty of many progressives' definition of internationalism. Instead of blindly touting the U.S. form of government as superior, they outlined its shortcomings in its domination of other nations, while at the same time suggesting an alternative way to conceptualize the world.

NYC-WPP ATTITUDES TOWARD
RACIAL INJUSTICE AND RACISM

Members of the NYC-WPP did not stop at criticizing women's subjugation to men but explored political, class, and racial oppression as well. Mygatt and Witherspoon often exposed the connected oppressions of sexism, racism, capitalism, and militarism in their work. *Four Lights* reported on racial violence, revealing connections between racism and militarism. In the 25 August 1917 issue, Ovington attacked President Wilson for his indifference toward the atrocities committed against African Americans during the East St. Louis riot in July 1917. "Six weeks have passed since the race riots of July and no public word of rebuke, no demand for the punishment of the offenders, has come from our Chief Executive," charged Ovington. "The American Negroes have died under more horrible conditions than any non-combatants who were sunk by German submarines. But to our President, their deaths do not merit consideration." American military troops exacerbated the race riots, reported Ovington. The NYC-WPP was the only peace group to make such charges publicly.[17]

Four Lights writers did not, however, analyze the racism inherent in the progressive dichotomy of "civilization" versus "barbarism." Florence Guertin Tuttle's poem "If" warned that the European war constituted "race annihilation," or the elimination of the white race through warfare. The New Yorkers also accepted the suffragist strategy of provoking white men's racist attitudes to obtain woman suffrage. In a series of questions under the heading, "Why Women Don't Fight," the editors asked, "What did American women win in the Civil War? The right of Negro men to vote." "American women" meant *white* women: *Four Lights* excluded African American women by conflating race and gender (white women) with nationality (American). The NYC-WPP reprinted an article entitled, "As Others See Us," by George Brandes, in which the author feared that the "yellow, brown and black" races would take advantage of the hostilities among the warring white race to win advantage for themselves. For all their radical ideas, *Four Lights* nonetheless reflected accepted nineteenth-century attitudes of white purity and "civilization." Still, the New York women stood alone among pacifist groups in making public their concern for racial injustice. In 1919, for example, the organization sponsored a Woman's Freedom Congress, which included a presentation on African American women's concerns.[18]

U.S. INTERVENTION, MILITARISM, AND SEXISM

Addressing the national WPP in their 21 April 1917 issue, the New York women suggested responses to the congressional declaration of war. The New Yorkers recommended battling against compulsory military training, warding off attacks against organized labor, and defending freedom of speech. The writers implored the WPP to "continue to take the long view, not to suffer from the illusion of the near." The feminists warned against "blind patriotism . . . that demands that America be first, [and] that since she is the greatest and richest country she shall dominate." The editors urged the United States to "lay down arms, and, turning to the international ideal, work for a world state."[19] The editors of *Four Lights* indeed took the long view, for merely to criticize the U.S. government for entering the war fell short of the group's goals. By looking past the present debate over intervention, the women predicted that one consequence of intervention, a "blind patriotism," would only hamper postwar moves toward internationalism.

After intervention the women began pressing the government to tell citizens exactly what its war aims were. Later, in bold letters, *Four Lights* asked, **"WHAT ARE THE WAR AIMS AND PEACE TERMS OF THE AMERICAN WOMEN? Why have we American women declared war on German women? What do we demand? Upon what terms will we make peace?"** With these questions, editors Mary Alden Hopkins and Elisabeth Irwin implored their readers to consider war a gendered issue. Their entreaties intensified the national WPP's initial call for the U.S. government to consult women on issues of war and peace. The New Yorkers reminded readers that the American democracy continued to ignore women's participation in matters of foreign policy.[20]

Four Lights also pointed out the oppressive nature of militarism. NYC-WPP member Eastman worked with other pacifists on the AUAM's campaign against military preparedness. The AUAM's class-based rhetoric argued that the propreparedness reasoning of progressives such as Ray Stannard Baker and Herbert Croly perpetuated a false notion of the United States as a nation of middle- and upper-class men grown lazy with too much leisure time and too much idle consumerism — deficiencies that military training (and, ultimately, war) would supposedly eradicate. The

NYC-WPP agreed with the AUAM's critique, but it probed the problem of militarism more deeply. The pages of *Four Lights* were filled with anecdotes, cartoons, and quotations revealing the sexist nature of militarism.

The issue that featured the petticoats and white feathers illustrations included an anecdote about "war heroes" recuperating at a hospital in Montreal. One of the convalescents described his leave-time escapades with two women he had picked up on the St. Lawrence Main. The soldier boasted of now having to "suffer the consequences" of his carouse. Then an eighteen-year-old soldier arrived, began drinking, and twenty minutes later started a brawl with the braggart. "All this," added Cleghorn sarcastically, "before he went to fight for 'King and Country.'" Cleghorn pointed out that while gender conformists praised soldiers for their heroism in the line of duty, *Four Lights* suggested that military service did not always produce praiseworthy men.[21]

But the women took issue with other pacifist journals as well. For example, in their most telling critique of militarism, the editors reprinted a commentary from *The Nation*, a journal owned by the pacifist Oswald Garrison Villard and later edited by *Four Lights* writer Kirchwey. *The Nation* described the sexual victimization of young women in Europe by victorious soldiers. "For her own sake she had better in the majority of cases be dead," contended *The Nation*. "'From the standpoint of the interests of society, she had much better be dead.'" In reprinting the article, *Four Lights* revealed the sexism and misogynism underlying the antiwar journalist's war report. Highly critical of the piece, the editors went on to say that "similar 'better dead than dishonor' statements were being constantly made in regard to the unfortunate women outraged by invading armies." This attitude "assumes as self-evident," maintained *Four Lights*, "*that a woman's honor concerns only this one function*. Men seem to be unanimous on this point. It would be enlightening to learn what proportion of women agree that 'From the standpoint of the interests of society she had much better be dead'" (emphasis added).[22]

MATERNALISM AND WAR

Four Lights writers also represented the concerns that mothers had for peace. Ovington and Anna Howard Shaw argued from essentialist positions in *Four Lights*, claiming that women alone repudiated war. "Women hate war," declared Ovington. "They hate the destruction of life with such intensity that they will never permit its continuance." Shaw maintained that after suffrage, women would likely vote against war.[23] Madeline Z.

Doty, however, went beyond the essentialist position. Her short story, entitled *"Die Mutter"* [The Mother] served two purposes; on the one hand, it expressed one of the theoretical links between feminism and pacifism that constituted the founding tenet of the national WPP — the notion that women desire peace because the fruits of their reproductive labor become the victims of war. But Doty also maintained that the prosecutors of war imposed militarism on innocent soldiers; in other words, the *military spirit was not inherent in male soldiers* but rather was created for political purposes. Doty thus expanded the importance of motherhood beyond the realm of personal experience, making maternity a politial position involving all of humanity.

"Die Mutter: A True Story" told of a young English pilot, distanced from the humanity of his target by the metal and wood of his aircraft, who killed the flyer of a German bomber. As he left his own plane's protective shell, the Englishman pulled his victim from the rubble and buried his face in grief. He found a photograph of the German's mother on the dead soldier, and a note the son had written to her. Doty described the German mother's feelings toward her dead son, which she projected onto all children: "All men are our sons. . . . I long to take you in my arms and lay your head upon my breast to make you feel through me your kinship with all the earth." Doty also made mothers responsible for the war, however: "Perhaps women more than men have been to blame for this world war. We did not think of the world's children, our children. The baby hands that clutched our breasts were so sweet, we forgot the hundred other baby hands stretched out to us. But the Earth does not forget, she mothers all." Here, the author warned that women must look beyond their personal experiences of motherhood. If their pacifism was to become truly revolutionary, they must care for "all the world's children."[24]

WAR-RELIEF WORK

Some suffragists not only accepted war but also participated in the conflict through war-relief work. Even before the U.S. Congress voted to declare war on Germany, the WPP and other women's groups, such as the National American Women Suffrage Association, debated the issue of war-relief work. Aiding government-sponsored programs to conserve food, enlisting as volunteers to roll Red Cross bandages, or visiting soldiers' hospitals involved women in the war effort. The women of the Massachusetts branch heartily endorsed such activities. By contrast, the NYC-WPP interpreted war work as "a vague desire to serve one's country [that] envelopes us on all sides. . . . It is very easy to fall in line with the masses and do [war work]," wrote the New Yorkers. "Meanwhile, more fundamental needs are neglected . . . we should enter into no sort of war work direct or indirect."[25] The New York feminists viewed war-relief work as the most crucial issue they faced after intervention.

In July 1917 New York Governor Charles Seymour Whitman ordered that a census determine the military resources of the state, including the availability of female residents to perform war-industry work. The NYC-WPP, which objected furiously to voluntary war-relief work, also repudiated paid war work. The NYC-WPP formed a separate committee to look into the matter. The Committee for Military Census of Women wondered why, when men answered the question — "Do you claim exemption from military service" — on their registration forms, women were not asked a similar question. Already facing charges of treason, the NYC-WPP complied with the governor's request but suggested that pacifist women note their objections on registration forms.[26]

The NYC-WPP also addressed relief work in *Four Lights*. Hopkins offered this mocking "advice" to women in "Woman's Ways in War":

Women feel that they cannot help in the Great War because they are accustomed to dealing with little things. Women must not feel that because they work in the narrow confines of the home, they cannot help in the great work of destruction. It is a tender nursery thought that the baby in the mother's arms, properly trained, may grow up to destroy more persons and property than any man before him. And that this helpless floppy pink hand may some day write his mother's name in the blood of the enemy. . . . Women have often been accused of being essentially producers and conservers. Now is the time for them to lay forever that slander and prove that they are glad and eager to destroy joyfully all that the ages — and other women — have produced. It takes but a minute to destroy a boy into whose making have gone eighteen years of thoughtful care.[27]

Hopkins addressed women's oppression under patriarchy in two ways. First, she contradicted the assumption that women's proper roles as mothers and wives prevented them from political activism. Second, she admonished women for using their life's work — keeping house and raising children — to perpetuate their own oppression and the destruction of their children on battlefields. War work only succeeded in bringing about the further oppression of women, by keeping them at home and by destroying the products of their labor.

Continuing the critique of relief efforts, the New Yorkers published their most inflammatory piece entitled "Sister Susie's Peril." Katherine Anthony left no doubt who "Sister Susie" was: the women on the WPP's national board and those in other branches, especially the Massachusetts branch, who knitted socks for soldiers. But Anthony broadened the argument, making war work a class *and* a feminist pacifist issue. She accused these "Sister Susies" of taking work away from self-supporting working women in the knitting mills and garment factories. Relief work, she said, was "a peculiarly infantile form of patriotism," a dumping of "unskill [*sic*] and inexperience on a disturbed labor market." Knitting socks was "infantile" because it was unnecessary. It was unnecessary because surely a government that could afford an arsenal of military equipment could purchase a sufficient number of socks for its soldiers.

The same issue reproduced a Lewis W. Hine photograph depicting a woman seated at a table, surrounded by five children who were making miniature flags with paper and paste. The mother held a baby in her lap. The editors described the photo's subjects as "involuntary scabettes of the war rang[ing] in age from ten to five. They are paid three cents . . . for sticking a pin into a tiny flag emblem to be worn in the buttonhole. The earnings of all, including the mother, come to two dollars a week." The editors implied that this particular family volunteered their labor out of patriotism, while unemployed workers, who needed money, were forced to go without. Moreover, patriots chided poor families who were unable to find employment, buy war bonds, or do relief work, by calling them "slackers." The editors ended their commentary on the picture with, "[T]he baby" seated on its mother's lap, "is a slacker."[28]

The NYC-WPP also attacked the suffragist strategy of joining the war effort. The 21 April 1917 issue included a poem entitled, "A Study in Evolution":

> And for your service and your sacrifice,
> Your heroism, self-denial, skill,
> Endurance, strength,
> Your nimble fingers shaping things that kill.
> We grant you votes.
> You speak the language that we understand,
> In these, our days of war.[29]

This poem used the sardonic wit with which *Four Lights* readers were familiar, in this case to condemn both war work and, particularly, the suffragists who eagerly signed up as volunteers. National WPP members believed they needed to justify themselves as war volunteers, but the NYC-WPP instead saw the exchange of war work for votes as a decidedly bad deal.

A CRITIQUE OF WARTIME AND
PROGRESSIVE LANGUAGE

The women of *Four Lights* were cognizant of how language operated in society, especially how language was "conscripted" during war:

A war that has scarcely begun has already achieved a sinister influence upon the words of our common speech. . . . Words that have had forced upon them an extraordinary igniting power are now successfully used as verbal fuses, even where their use is utterly paradoxical. Conspicuous among these, of course, [is the word] "democracy." A war instigated in the name of national vengeance is now declared to be a fight for "Democracy." Many docile-minded persons are acquiescing in the policy of conscription because they are assured it is "democratic." The slaughter, starvation and utter humiliation of a foreign people is urged as a means of converting it to "Democracy." The word "peace," recently conscripted, has likewise come to find itself in the strange company of the words "force" and "courage" and is now used to describe the attitude of persons who think and act with the majority. Quite as significant, perhaps, is the interned word . . . "liberty."[30]

In this piece, Olivia Howard Dunbar exposed the hypocrisy behind Woodrow Wilson's phrase, "to make the world safe for democracy."[31]

In the 30 June 1917 issue, the editors uncovered the dangers of two other progressive bywords, "efficiency" and "virtue." Claiming that German people had not created militarism, Marjorie Benton Cooke wrote, "It [Prussianism] expresses itself in autocracy, in the exploitation of labor by capital, *in the deification of efficiency*, in the might-makes-right idea, in hideous cruelty, justified by virtuous ends; ergo, national self-defence; ergo, patriotism." Cooke mocked one of the most cherished progressive ideals by insinuating that progressives' emphasis on efficiency came perilously close to the very aspect of German civilization — militarism — they claimed to be fighting to eradicate. In his article on compulsory military training, Henry Neumann complained that "[W]hat is wanted now is an America subservient, made docile in the name of efficiency, submissive in the name of preparedness, drilled into automatic obedience to an upper class in the name of patriotism." Both Cooke and Neumann insinuated that American culture featured some of the very attributes the U.S. military fought to extinguish in the enemy.[32]

THE END OF *FOUR LIGHTS*

On 15 June 1917, lawmakers passed the Espionage Act, which authorized the Postal Service to withhold mail it deemed subversive. When the postmaster declared two issues of *Four Lights* treasonous, the Post Office refused to deliver these editions. The 2 June and 30 June 1917 issues contained clippings from another censored journal, the socialist *New York Call*, and a Randolph Bourne essay critical of George Creel, whom President Wilson had appointed to head the propaganda arm of the war effort. The women made inquiries regarding the censorship, but the Post Office did not respond to their questions. *Four Lights* ceased publication after October 1917. A special 12 June 1919 edition covered the International Congress of Women in Zurich, a meeting which paralleled the Paris peace conference. During the Zurich gathering, the Woman's Peace Party became the U.S. section of the Women's International League for Peace and Freedom (WILPF). The 1919 *Four Lights* issue was the last, until the WILPF resurrected the journal in the 1940s.[33]

The journal suspended publication between October 1917 and June 1919 for several reasons. After the treason charge, the NYC-WPP discovered that because its account books had not been accurately kept, it was floundering in debt. When New York women won the vote in November 1917, the NYC-WPP became the New York state branch of the WPP, hoping to increase membership and pay its bills. The NYC-WPP halted its criticisms of the president and praised his January 1918 speech before Congress, in which he outlined his plans for peace. This aligned the New Yorkers more closely with their parent organization. But such positive feelings regarding the peace settlement were short-lived.[34]

CONTROVERSIAL CHANGES
IN NAME AND STRATEGY

The New Yorkers rejoiced when their state passed woman suffrage. But the censorship of the NYC-WPP's journal affected the women's goals and strategies to an even greater degree. Shortly after the state branch formed, chairman Crystal Eastman authored a defensive and erroneous piece titled "Our War Record," in which she claimed that the New Yorkers had ceased opposing the war after intervention and instead began focusing on affecting the peace settlement. This document mirrored the reasons President Wilson cited for intervening in the war: that Americans would have to join the war in order to be allowed "a seat at the peace table." Some of the actions taken by the NYC-WPP reflected Eastman's claims; yet in other ways, the New York branch retained its radical tone and agenda.[35]

In June 1918 the New York state WPP voted in favor of changing its name to the Women's International League (WIL). Opinions about the name change varied. Members preferring the new name stated that the group decided to stop opposing the war at its 1918 convention. "If there is a body of women, ready to oppose the war actively now and suffer the inevitable swift penalty," wrote those in favor of WIL, "Woman's Peace Party might well be their name. But it is not rightly *our* name. It does not describe what we are doing, nor what the majority of us believe in doing, while the war is on." Those wishing to keep the name "Woman's Peace Party" said that they wanted to exclude those opposed to the word "peace"; furthermore, they did *not* want to cease the organization's stop-the-war activity. Nevertheless, caution ruled the day, and the New York state WPP became the Women's International League.[36]

After the warring nations began deliberating the settlement terms in 1919, the New Yorkers again shifted gears. In March 1919 WIL organized a "Woman's Freedom Congress," which included presentations on topics such as "Women Workers," "Labor Legislation for Women," "The Future of the Colored Woman," and "Birth Control, the Illegitimate Child, and Related Subjects." Notable speakers included Rose Schneiderman of the Women's Trade Union League, radical Industrial Workers of the World leader Elizabeth Gurley Flynn, and Minnie Brown of the National Association for the Advancement of Colored People. Organizers of the Woman's Freedom Congress hoped participants would sense the power of working together to benefit *all* women across race and class boundaries.[37]

Two other postwar documents reflected a rejuvinated desire to use the word "peace." In May 1919 members of the International Congress of Women assembled in Zurich to write a counter-document to the treaty signed by representatives from warring nations. To these women, the WIL offered its support, stating emphatically, "We are pacifists — pacifists in war-time as well as pacifists in peace-time."

Later in May 1919, the WIL issued a statement blasting the Treaty of Versailles. The women proclaimed that the war to end all wars had proved a failure. In 1915, recalled the women, the Woman's Peace Party had united with pacifist women of the Allied countries, the Central European Powers, and the neutral nations, in order "to hasten peace and secure a democratic settlement. *We failed, not because we were wrong, but because we had no power.*" The WIL acknowledged that men who "have no respect for human life, or for the counsel and needs of women" still controlled the world. The feminists then pledged to defeat the "war-breeding" Treaty of Versailles, an agreement that punished Germany harshly. The WIL advocated a treaty that spurned indemnities and annexations and demanded the complete disarmament of all nations. To build "**A SANE WORLD ORDER**," they wrote in bold capital letters, "**WE [WOMEN] MUST HAVE FREEDOM IN EVERY FIELD OF ACTIVITY AND THE POWER THAT FREEDOM BRINGS. IN THE STRUGGLE FOR OUR EMANCIPATION WE HAVE NOT DESTROYED A SINGLE LIFE. BY AIDING MEN TO RELEASE THEMSELVES FROM THEIR BONDAGE TO VIOLENCE AND BLOODSHED WE SHALL ALSO FREE OURSELVES, FOR WOMEN CAN NEVER KNOW TRUE LIBERTY IN A SOCIETY DOMINATED BY FORCE.**" In this document, the WIL expressed the essentialist strategies voiced by the early women's peace movement: that women, as morally superior to men, oppose war and are by nature nonviolent. Judging by the Woman's Freedom Congress they sponsored, the WIL believed that "freedom" meant the ability to pursue economic independence, education, and reproductive rights. Without such freedoms, the women could not foresee gaining any power in a society dominated by force. Along the way, however, feminists would have to rid society of bloodshed and violence; otherwise they could not "know true liberty."[38]

The WPP's 1915 platform argued that women — and their domestic or "private" sphere — were equally important as men's "public" sphere of business, industry, and politics. They demanded women be *given* an equal share in deciding the questions of war and peace. In 1919 members of the WIL admitted that they did not share power equally with men and were not yet "emancipated" from women's servile position within society. Men had failed to forge a "sane world order" during the peace negotiations: they could not, because they were still mired in "violence and bloodshed." At its inception in 1914, the WPP had perceived pacifist men as "very masculine" in outlook, having little respect for women. By 1919, WIL members were ready to "emancipate" themselves from their subservient roles, not by asking men for recognition but by preparing themselves — pursuing education, economic independence, and reproductive freedom — to *take* power for themselves.

Much had changed between 1915 and 1919. The United States intervened in the Great War, stopped fighting in 1918, and helped write a peace treaty in 1919. The New York City WPP published *Four Lights*, defended it to the Postal Service, voted for the first time, rejoiced when combat abated, formulated plans for an acceptable peace, and then watched as world leaders' ideas regarding the settlement, which differed from their own, were implemented. These events both sobered and radicalized the

New Yorkers. Some members understandably worried about the treason charge. Women whose livelihood depended on their jobs feared reprisal. Others, who were not dependent on paychecks, nevertheless did not want to lose meaningful positions or the ability to pursue other work in the future. "It is undesirable," admitted the New York WPP when it confronted Governor Whitman's women's census registration, "to disobey the laws of this state."[39]

But the Great War and the pursuit of peace had energized feminist pacifists as well. If in 1915 they had hoped to be offered a chance to determine the question of war and peace, their experiences during the debate over war, and regarding the peace settlement process, suggested that equality would not be forthcoming. For the New Yorkers, peace or "true liberty" and a "sane world order" seemed a long way off in 1919, given women's relatively powerless position. While suffrage in some sense validated their political activism and provided greater access to candidates, access alone did not empower them.

In 1914 two New Yorkers, Eastman and Doty, were responsible for founding the first feminist pacifist organization in U.S. history. Without the New Yorkers' confrontational attitude toward militarism and the Wilson administration's war effort, censorship under the Espionage Act and the New York military census laws would not have drawn fire from the women's peace movement. Older-generation peace activists did not view the war or war-relief work as critically as did the New York feminists. As Ellen Carol Dubois noted, younger progressive women did not cling to women's traditional sphere as did many older-generation WPP members. Most of the women of the NYC-WPP were the "free lances" Lillian Wald described, tethered neither to a "respectable" marriage nor to an institution.[40] As such, they felt freer to pursue unconventional roles and radical ideas about war and society. The NYC-WPP's goals — to obliterate the connected oppressions it saw and experienced in society, and which it believed exacerbated militarism — differed from the objectives of the national WPP dominated by the older generation. The NYC-WPP's discourse was indeed exhilarating, as Barbara Sicherman noted, but no more so than involvement in war-relief work was for the national WPP. Older pacifists, such as Fanny Garrison Villard, Jane Addams, Lucia Ames Mead, Lillian Wald, and Rose Dabney Forbes, provided needed leadership, financial resources, and a history of women's rights activism, all necessary ingredients during the fledgling feminist peace movement's early years.

NOTES

1. Nancy S. Dye, "Introduction," in *Gender, Class, Race and Reform in the Progressive Era*, ed. Nancy S. Dye and Noralee Frankel (Lexington: University of Kentucky Press, 1991), 1–9; Ellen Carol Dubois, "Harriot Stanton Blatch and the Transformation of Class Relations Among Women Suffragists," in *Gender, Class, Race and Reform in the Progressive Era*, ed. Nancy S. Dye and Noralee Frankel (Lexington: University of Kentucky Press, 1991), 162–179; "Preamble and Platform, January 10, 1915," SR 12.1, WPP Papers, SCPC.

2. Barbara Sicherman, "Working it Out: Gender, Profession and Reform in the Career of Alice Hamilton," in *Gender, Class, Race and Reform in the Progressive Era*, ed. Nancy S. Dye and Noralee Frankel (Lexington: University of Kentucky Press, 1991), 141.

3. See Barbara J. Steinson, *American Women's Activism in World War I* (New York: Garland Press, 1982), 299–349 for a description of women's involvement in the war effort. Many women in the Women's Section of the Navy League complained that they were not treated respectfully, especially by Secretary of the Navy Josephus Daniels. Steinson also notes prejudice against women volunteers.

4. Many antisuffrage women also joined the war effort; see Barbara J. Steinson's chapter 7, "The Women's Relief, Preparedness and Suffrage Movements Go to War," in ibid., 299–349.

5. Judith Schwarz, *Radical Feminists of Heterodoxy: Greenwich Village 1912–1940* (Norwich, Vt.: New Victoria Publishers, 1986), offers short biographies of each member of Heterodoxy in Appendix C, pp. 116–128 but notes that she has been unable to get complete information on all members. *Four Lights*, 28 July 1917, SR 23.01, WPP Papers, SCPC.

6. *Four Lights*, 27 January 1917.

7. Ibid., 14 July 1917; ibid., 27 January 1917.

8. Ibid., 27 January 1917.

9. This letter appears in the *Four Lights* microfilm.

10. *Four Lights*, 6 February 1917; "A People's Referendum"; ibid., 24 February 1917.

11. See Walton Rawls, *Wake Up America! World War I and the American Poster* (New York: Abbeville Press, 1988), 124–129, 152, 160, for reproductions of Red Cross posters; *Four Lights*, 14 July 1917.

12. *Four Lights*, 2 June 1917.

13. Edna Kenton, "North, South, East, West," *Four Lights*, 27 January 1917.

14. A.D., "Friendly Relations Commissions," *Four Lights*, 7 February 1917.

15. *Four Lights*, 6 February 1917. The editors of the 16 June issue boxed off a quote by Ralph Waldo Emerson to help them articulate a definition of acceptable nationalism: "If you have a nation of men who have risen to that height of

moral cultivation that they will not declare war or carry arms, for they have not so much madness left in their brains, you have a nation of lovers, of benefactors, of true, great and able men. Let me know more of that nation." Under the box, they featured statements in the *Congressional Record*: "History proves that the rate of advancement of civilization and political liberty has been in proportion to the degree of freedom of speech and the press, exercised in their behalf, and that without these principal factors we should not have attained democracy or a republican form of government" (Moses F. Kincaid statement, 4 May 1917).

16.   *Four Lights*, 10 March 1917.

17.   Nancy Manahan, "Future Old Maids and Pacifist Agitators; The Story of Tracy Mygatt and Francis Witherspoon," *Women's Studies Quarterly* 10 (Spring 1982): 10–13; Mary White Ovington, *Four Lights*, 25 August 1917.

18.   Florence Guertin Tuttle, "If," *Four Lights*, 28 July 1917; "Why Women Don't Fight," *Four Lights*, 14 July 1917; George Brandes, "As Others See Us," *Four Lights*, 21 April 1917; "Women Freedom Congress" flyer, SR 12.4, WPP Papers, SCPC.

19.   *Four Lights*, 21 April 1917.

20.   Ibid., 14 July 1917.

21.   Ibid., 6 February 1917.

22.   Ibid., 14 July 1917.

23.   Ibid., 21 April 1917; ibid., 24 February 1917.

24.   Mary White Ovington, "What We May Do To-day," *Four Lights*, 21 April 1917; Anna Howard Shaw, "Votes for Women," *Four Lights*, 24 February 1917; Madeline Z. Doty, *"Die Mutter*: A True Story," *Four Lights*, 24 March 1917.

25.   "On War Work," anonymous group, but clearly NYC-WPP, (n.d.) S.R. 12.1, Box 1, WPP Papers, SCPC.

26.   Press release, 11 June 1917, New York state WPP, SR 12.4, WPP Papers, SPCP.

27.   Mary Alden Hopkins, "Women's Ways in War," *Four Lights*, 2 June 1917.

28.   *Four Lights*, 14 July 1917.

29.   A. B. Curtis, "A Study in Evolution; From Mr. Asquith and the British Government," *Four Lights*, 21 April 1917.

30.   Olivia Howard Dunbar, "Conscripted Words," *Four Lights*, 5 May 1917.

31.   Ibid.

32.   Marjorie Benton Cooke, "Of the Spirit," *Four Lights*, 30 June 1917; Henry Neumann, "Compulsory Military Training," *Four Lights*, 21 April 1917.

33.   Press release, 16 July 1917, NYC-WPP, SR 12.4, WPP Papers, SCPC; George Creel to F. Witherspoon, 16 July 1917, G. Creel to M. Lane, 12 July 1917, M. Lane to G. Creel, 7 July 1917, SR 12.4, WPP Papers, SCPC; "Malone Aids Fight of Anti-Draft Press," *New York Times*, 14 July 1917, 14; Harriet Hyman Alonso, *Peace as a Women's Issue: A History of the U.S. Movement for*

World Peace and Women's Rights (Syracuse, N.Y.: Syracuse University Press, 1993), 83; the entire run of *Four Lights*, including the 1940s version, is on reels 23.01–23.05, housed at SCPC.

34. Elinor Byrns to Dear Board Member, 16 May 1919, SR 12.4, WPP Papers, SCPC; Acting Secretary to Fannie Witherspoon, 16 October 1917, SR 12.4, WPP Papers, SCPC; *New York Times*, 13 January 1918, 18; *New York Times*, 3 February 1918, 3.

35. Crystal Eastman, "Our War Record," 21 December 1917, SR 12.4, WPP Papers, SCPC.

36. "Shall We Change the Name?" SR 12.4, WPP Papers, SPCP.

37. Convention Committee to Dear Friend, 15 Feb 1919, SR 12.4, WPP Papers, SCPC; "Woman's Freedom Congress" flyer, SR 12.4, WPP Papers, SCPC.

38. Chairman to Members of the International Committee of Women for Permanent Peace, 22 April 1919, SR 12.4, WPP Papers, SCPC; "Women's International League," 29 May 1919, SR 12.4, WPP Papers, SCPC.

39. Executive Board to Member, 12 June 1917, SR 12.4, WPP Papers, SCPC.

40. Wald quoted in C. Roland Marchand, *The American Peace Movement and Social Reform, 1898–1918* (Princeton, N.J.: Princeton University Press, 1972), 259.

Conclusion

A few days after Representative Jeannette Rankin voted against the war declaration in Congress, she received an acerbic condemnation from a constituent. "So, you have acted just as I have always said women would act when they THINK they can stand in men's shoes. . . . If you think yourself fitted to fill a man's place in the political world," wrote the Montanan, "then, for Heaven's sake, FILL IT as a man would or get out and make room for another who has a little will-power. Among the lawmakers of our country there is no place for weakness." The constituent, who identified herself simply as "A WOMAN VOTER," expressed the belief of a majority of U.S. lawmakers: that in public matters of foreign policy, repudiation of war signaled weakness, and weakness — which the letter-writer equated with femininity and pacifism — proved anathema to congressmen who insisted on bolstering the nation's manhood through combat.[1]

Most lawmakers — whether pro-war or antiwar — framed the president's war declaration as a legal matter of public policy to which they voiced their dutiful consent. Positing war as a civic duty enabled them to exclude women from the debate for two reasons: First, because with the exception of some western states politicians did not represent disenfranchised women, and second, because women's presumed domestic sphere kept them out of the public realm. This public-male versus private-female dichotomy reinforced the notion that male combatants strengthened democracy, whereas feminist pacifists weakened it.

Gender conformity constituted a powerful tool used to solidify progressive hegemony in support of war. Masculine strength was implied in the progressive ideology of internationalism; it became one of the most crucial reasons for progressives' advocacy of military preparedness and, ultimately, formed the primary justification for intervention. After the war declaration, all segments of society mobilized to join the war effort — male combatants and industrial workers, female recruits, laborers, and relief volunteers — and were called upon to participate in ways that reinforced conventional masculinity and femininity. Wartime propagandists, however, did little to recruit citizens of color, regardless of gender.

If ideas of gender were among the most persuasive factors encouraging progressives to support intervention, then those peace organizations ignoring gender did so at their peril. The World Peace Foundation's (WPF) founder Edwin Ginn believed that educating the masses would prevent war. Part of the WPF's education program rested on the notion of American superiority relative to other nations. When the United States began supporting military preparedness and then intervention in the European war, the WPF backed both policies.

The American Union Against Militarism (AUAM) organized in order to prevent the United States from preparing militarily for war. These socialists and social workers argued that the wealthy classes—specifically arms manufacturers, newspaper owners, and bankers—created the preparedness hysteria and then sounded the call for intervention. The AUAM claimed to speak for the oppressed classes, whom it viewed as victims of upper-class hawkishness. The class argument, which mirrored most accurately the arguments put forth by lawmakers such as U.S. senators Robert LaFollette and George Norris, neglected the persuasive power of gender conformity used by the pro-war faction to gain support for war. Thus, when interventionist arguments became masculine, some AUAM members, such as Edward Devine, joined the pro-war camp.

The Woman's Peace Party (WPP) originated when women sensed that male pacifists were doing nothing to stop the European war. They claimed that women were the victims of war and should therefore have a say in determining when and whether the nation should enter the conflict. Some within the WPP argued that women were the exclusive moral standard bearers in American society and that if women held political power, there would be no more wars. But as the nation chose a militarist path in the face of the European war, the WPP's public statements became less and less reflective of the essentialist feminist position they had trumpeted earlier. The WPF, the AUAM, and the WPP did not address the allure of male comradeship, which tantalized so many progressives.

The New York City WPP's (NYC-WPP) probing critique of the potency of gender conformity, and of the racism and classism they viewed as inherent in a militaristic society, pierced the progressives' consensus for intervention. The NYC-WPP confronted progressive hegemony by inverting the ideology of reform. The progressive efficiency cult had actually *re*gressed, according to the New Yorkers, to the point where it rivaled "Prussianism" in its insistence on conformity. The progressive practice of coalition-building was merely a facade enabling elitists to retain power. The women also chipped away at the power of progressive pacifist ideology. Internationalism masqueraded as a euphemism for American domination, and pacifists' concern for femininity ravaged by victorious soldiers masked an assumption that women's only use to men — and, therefore, to the rest of society — was as sex objects. Thus, the women's experiences during World War I severely diminished their faith in progressive reform. Furthermore, despite their insightful gendered discourse, the NYC-WPP had had little impact on the congressional debate that resulted in war.

Some New York pacifists reasoned that woman suffrage would reduce the likelihood of another armed conflict. Anna Howard Shaw and other *Four Lights* writers insisted that when granted suffrage women voters would uniformly reject war.[2] Rankin's Montana constituent quickly dispelled this notion when she blasted the pacifist's vote as "weak." New York women entered voting booths themselves shortly after intervention. They soon discovered, however, that woman suffrage did not alter the content or tone of the "war-breeding" Treaty of Versailles. The peace treaty convinced the women that the women's peace movement had failed because women lacked real power. Broadening the base of activism through the empowerment of women — significantly, across class and race boundaries — became the group's next project in the postwar era.

NOTES

1. "A woman voter" to Miss Rankin, 9 April 1917, Box 12, folder 6, Rankin Collection, Montana Historical Society, Helena, Montana.

2. Anna Howard Shaw, "Votes for Women," *Four Lights*, 24 February 1917, SR 23.01, WPP Papers, SCPC.

Selected Bibliography

PRIMARY SOURCES

Manuscript Collections

Swarthmore College Peace Collection (SCPC), Swarthmore, Pa.:
     American Union Against Militarism (AUAM) Papers
     Emergency Peace Federation (EPF) Papers
     Woman's Peace Party (WPP) Papers
     World Peace Foundation (WPF) Papers
Montana Historical Society, Helena, Mont.:
     Jeannette Rankin Papers

Published Documents

Report of the Joint Legislative Committee Investigating Seditious Activities, Filed April 24, 1920, in the Senate of the State of New York: Revolutionary Radicalism. Pt. 1, Vol. 1. Clayton R. Lusk, chairman. Albany: J. B. Lyon Co., Printers, 1920.
Congressional Record. 65th Congress, special session, 1917.

Newspapers and Periodicals

The Appeal to Reason
Chicago Tribune
Four Lights
Independent
New Republic
New York Times
North American Review
Outlook
San Francisco Chronicle
Survey
Washington Post
World's Work

Books

Addams, Jane. *Peace and Bread in Time of War.* 1922. Reprint. Silver Spring, Md.: National Association of Social Workers, 1983.

____. *Second Twenty Years at Hull House, September 1909 to September 1929.* New York: Macmillan, 1930.

Bourne, Randolph S. *The War and the Intellectuals.* New York: American Union Against Militarism, 1917.

Christy, Howard Chandler. *The American Girl.* 1906. Reprint. New York: DaCapo, 1976.

Coolidge, Mary Roberts. *Why Women Are So.* 1912. Reprint. New York: Arno Press, 1972.

Department of Labor Research. *American Labor Year Book, 1917.* New York: Rand School of Social Science, 1917.

Hudson, Maxim. *Defenseless America.* New York: Hearst's International Library Co., 1915.

Jordan, David Starr. *The Days of a Man: Volume Two: 1900–1921.* Yonkers-on-Hudson, N.Y.: World Book Co., 1922.

Royce, Josiah. *The Duties of Americans in the Present War: Address Delivered at Tremont Temple, January 30, 1916.* New York: Citizens' League for America and Allies, 1916.

Shaw, Albert. *The Outlook for the Average Man.* New York: Macmillan, 1907.

Articles and Essays

Deland, Margaret. "The Changes in the Feminine Ideal." *Atlantic Monthly,* March 1910, 289–302.

Devine, Edward. "Ourselves and Europe: I." *Survey,* 4 November 1916, 99–100.

Hayes, Carleton J. "Which? War Without a Purpose? Or Armed Neutrality with a Purpose?" *Survey*, 10 February 1917, 535–538.

Holt, Hamilton. "The Crisis." *Independent*, 12 March 1917, 434.

"How Pacifists Mobilized Against War." *Survey*, 10 February 1917, 538.

Kellogg, Paul U. "The Fighting Issues." *Survey*, 17 February 1917, 573–574.

"Public Opinion and The War." *New Republic*, 21 April 1917, 334–336.

Rogers, Anna A. "Why American Marriages Fail." *Atlantic Monthly*, September 1907, 289–298.

Roosevelt, Theodore. "Democracy and Military Preparation: The Ideal." *Outlook*, 25 November 1914, 663–666.

____. "The Army for a Democracy." *Outlook*, 30 December 1914, 986–988.

"Socialists and the Problem of War: A Symposium." *Intercollegiate Socialist* 5 (April–May 1917): 7–27.

Stewart, Herbert L. "The Ethics of Luxury and Leisure." *American Journal of Sociology* 24 (November 1918): 241–259.

Thompson, Flora McDonald. "The Retrogression of the American Woman." *North American Review* 171 (November 1900): 748–753.

"Who Willed American Participation." *New Republic*, 14 April 1917, 308–310.

Wilcox, Ella Wheeler. "The Restlessness of the Modern Woman." *Cosmopolitan* 31 (July 1901): 314–317.

SECONDARY SOURCES

Books

Adamson, Walter L. *Hegemony and Revolution: A Study of Antonio Gramsci's Political and Cultural Theory*. Berkeley: University of California Press, 1980.

Alonso, Harriet Hyman. *Peace as a Women's Issue: A History of the U.S. Movement for World Peace and Women's Rights*. Syracuse, N.Y.: Syracuse University Press, 1993.

Arnett, Alex Mathews. *Claude Kitchin and the Wilson War Policies*. Boston: Little, Brown and Co., 1937.

Asher, Herbert B. *Freshmen Representatives and the Learning of Voting Cues*. Beverly Hills, Calif.: Sage Publications, 1973.

Bauer, Dale M., and Susan Jaret McKinstry, eds. *Feminism, Bakhtin and the Dialogic*. New York: State University of New York Press, 1991.

Bederman, Gail. *Manliness and Civilization: A Cultural History of Gender and Race in the United States, 1880–1917*. Chicago: University of Chicago Press, 1995.

Bolt, Ernest C. *Ballots Before Bullets: The War Referendum Approach to Peace in America, 1914–1941*. Charlottesville: University Press of Virginia, 1977.

Brock, Peter. *Pacifism in the United States: From the Colonial Era to the First World War*. Princeton, N.J.: Princeton University Press, 1968.

Buenker, John D., and Edward R. Kantowicz. *Historical Dictionary of the Progressive Era, 1890–1920*. Westport, Conn.: Greenwood Press, 1988.

Carroll, Berenice, et al. *The Role of Women in Conflict and Peace: Papers*. Ann Arbor: University of Michigan, Center for Continuing Education of Women, 1977.

Chamberlin, Hope. *A Minority of Members: Women in the U.S. Congress*. New York: Praeger Publishers, 1973.

Chambers, Clarke A. *Paul U. Kellogg and the Survey: Voices for Social Welfare and Social Justice*. Minneapolis: University of Minnesota Press, 1971.

Chambers, John Whiteclay, II, ed. *The Eagle and the Dove: The American Peace Movement and U.S. Foreign Policy, 1900–1922*, 2nd ed. Syracuse, N.Y.: Syracuse University Press, 1991.

Chatfield, Charles. *For Peace and Justice: Pacifism in America, 1914–1941*. Knoxville: University of Tennessee Press, 1971.

Conlin, Joseph R., ed. *American Anti-War Movements*. Beverly Hills, Calif.: Glencoe Press, 1968.

Cooper, Helen M., Adrienne Auslander Munich, and Susan Merrill Squier, eds. *Arms and the Woman: War, Gender, and Literary Representation*. Chapel Hill: University of North Carolina Press, 1989.

Cooper, John Milton, Jr. *The Vanity of Power: American Isolationism and the First World War, 1914–1917*. Westport, Conn.: Greenwood Press, 1969.

Coss, Clare, ed. *Lillian D. Wald: Progressive Activist*. New York: Feminist Press at City University of New York, 1989.

Cott, Nancy. *The Grounding of Modern Feminism*. New Haven: Yale University Press, 1987.

Curti, Merle. *Peace or War: The American Struggle, 1636–1936*. New York: W. W. Norton, 1936.

DeBennedetti, Charles. *Origins of the American Peace Movement, 1915–1929.* Millwood, N.Y.: KTO Press, 1978.

Degen, Marie Louise. *A History of the Woman's Peace Party*. 1939. Reprint. New York: Garland Press, 1972.

Douglas, Ann. *Terrible Honesty: Mongrel Manhattan in the 1920s*. New York: Farrar, Straus and Giroux, 1995.

Dye, Nancy S., and Noralee Frankel, eds. *Gender, Class, Race and Reform in the Progressive Era*. Lexington: University of Kentucky Press, 1991.

Eastman, Crystal. *Crystal Eastman on Women and Revolution*. Edited by Blanche Wiesen Cook. New York: Oxford University Press, 1978.

Edelman, Murray. *Constructing the Political Spectacle*. Chicago: University of Chicago Press, 1988.

Elshtain, Jean Bethke. *Woman and War*. New York: Basic Books, 1987.

Enloe, Cynthia. *Does Khaki Become You? The Militarisation of Women's Lives*. London: Pluto, 1983.

Femia, Joseph V. *Gramsci's Political Thought: Hegemony, Consciousness and the Revolutionary Process*. Oxfordshire: Clarendon Press, 1981.

Filene, Peter. *Him/Her/Self: Sex Roles in Modern America*, 2nd ed. Baltimore: Johns Hopkins University Press, 1986.

Forgacs, David, and Geoffrey Nowell Smith, eds. *Antonio Gramsci: Selections from Cultural Writings*. Trans. by William Boelhower. London: Lowell and Wishart, 1986.

Giddens, Anthony. *The Class Structure of Advanced Societies*, 2nd ed. London: Hutchinson, 1981.

Giles, Kevin S. *Flight of the Dove: The Story of Jeannette Rankin*. Beaverton, Ore.: Touchstone Press, 1980.

Gilligan, Carol. *In a Different Voice: Psychological Theory and Women's Development*. Cambridge: Harvard University Press, 1982.

Gramsci, Antonio. *Selections from the Prison Notebooks*. Edited and translated by Quintin Hoare and Geoffrey Nowell Smith. New York: International Publishers, 1971.

Greene, Theodore P. *America's Heroes: The Changing Models of Success in American Magazines*. New York: Oxford University Press, 1970.

Haber, Samuel. *Efficiency and Uplift: Scientific Management in the Progressive Era, 1890–1920*. Chicago: University of Chicago Press, 1964.

Harris, Adrienne, and Ynestra King, eds. *Rocking the Ship of State: Toward a Feminist Peace Politics*. San Francisco: Westview, 1989.

Herman, Sondra. *Eleven Against War: Studies in American Internationalism, 1898–1921*. Stanford, Calif.: Hoover Institution Press, 1969.

Higonnet, Margaret Randolph, Jane Jenson, Sonya Michel, and Margaret Collins Weitz. *Behind the Lines: Gender and the Two World Wars*. New Haven: Yale University Press, 1987.

Hinckley, Barbara. *The Seniority System in Congress*. Bloomington: Indiana University Press, 1971.

Holquist, Michael, ed. *Dialogic Imagination: Four Essays by Mikhail M. Bakhtin*. Translated by Caryl Emerson and Michael Holquist. Austin: University of Texas Press, 1981.

Howlett, Charles F. *The American Peace Movement: References and Resources*. Boston: G. K. Hall, 1991.

Howlett, Charles F., and Glen Zeitzer. *The American Peace Movement: History and Historiography*. Washington, D.C.: American Historical Association, 1985.

Josephson, Hannah. *Jeannette Rankin: First Lady in Congress*. New York: Bobbs-Merrill Co., 1974.

Josephson, Harold, ed. *Biographical Dictionary of Modern Peace Leaders*. Westport, Conn.: Greenwood Press, 1985.

Kolko, Gabriel. *The Triumph of Conservatism: A Reinterpretation of American History*. New York: Free Press, 1968.

Kraditor, Aileen. *Ideas of the Women Suffrage Movement, 1890–1920*. New York: Columbia University Press, 1965.

Kraft, Barbara S. *The Peace Ship: Henry Ford's Pacifist Adventure in the First World War*. New York: Macmillan, 1978.

Kuehl, Warren F. *Hamilton Holt: Journalist, Internationalist, Educator*. Gainesville: University of Florida Press, 1980.

Lengyel, Emil. *And All Her Paths Were Peace: The Life of Bertha von Suttner*. New York: Thomas Nelson, 1975.

Link, Arthur S. *Woodrow Wilson: Revolution, War and Peace*. Arlington Heights, Ill.: Harlan Davidson, 1979.

____. *Woodrow Wilson: Campaigns for Peace and Progressivism, 1916–1917*. Princeton, N.J.: Princeton University Press, 1965.

____. *Woodrow Wilson and the Progressive Era, 1910–1917*. New York: Harper, 1954.

Marchand, C. Roland. *The American Peace Movement and Social Reform, 1898–1918*. Princeton, N.J.: Princeton University Press, 1972.

May, Henry. *The End of American Innocence: A Study of the First Years of Our Own Time, 1912–1917*. New York: Knopf, 1959.

Nash, Roderick, ed. *The Call of the Wild, 1900–1916*. New York: Braziller, 1970.

Noble, David W. *The Progressive Mind, 1890–1917*. Chicago: Rand McNally, 1970.

Oleszek, Walter J. *Congressional Procedures and the Policy Process*, 2nd ed. Washington, D.C.: Congressional Quarterly Press, 1984.

Peterson, H. C., and Gilbert C. Fite. *Opponents of War, 1917–1918*. Madison: University of Wisconsin Press, 1957.

Pierson, Ruth Roach, ed. *Women and Peace: Theoretical, Historical and Practical Perspectives*. London: Croom Helm, 1987.

Randall, Mercedes M. *Improper Bostonian: Emily Greene Balch*. New York: Twayne, 1964.

Rawls, Walton. *Wake Up, America! World War I and the American Poster*. New York: Abbeville Press, 1988.

Roberts, Nancy L., ed. *American Peace Writers, Editors, and Periodicals*. Westport, Conn.: Greenwood Press, 1991.

Ruddick, Sara. *Maternal Thinking: Toward a Politics of Peace*. Boston: Beacon Press, 1989.

Schneider, Dorothy, and Carl J. Schneider. *American Women in the Progressive Era, 1900–1920*. New York: Facts on File, 1992.

Schwarz, Judith. *Radical Feminists of Heterodoxy: Greenwich Village, 1912–1940*. Norwich, Vt.: New Victoria Publishers, 1986.

Scott, Joan Wallach. *Gender and the Politics of History*. New York: Columbia University Press, 1988.

Sewall, May Wright. *Women, World War, and Permanent Peace*. 1915. Reprint. Westport, Conn.: Hyperion, 1976.

Showalter, Elaine, ed. *These Modern Women: Autobiographical Essays from the Twenties.* Old Westbury, N.Y.: Feminist Press, 1978.

Simon, Roger. *Gramsci's Political Thought: An Introduction.* London: Lawrence and Wishart, 1982.

Sochen, June. *The New Woman: Feminism in Greenwich Village, 1910–1920.* New York: Quadrangle Books, 1972.

Steinson, Barbara J. *American Women's Activities in World War I.* New York: Garland Press, 1982.

Thelen, David P. *Robert M. La Follette and the Insurgent Spirit.* Boston: Little, Brown and Co., 1976.

Thompson, John A. *Reformers and War: American Progressive Publicists and the First World War.* Cambridge: Cambridge University Press, 1987.

Todorov, Tzvetan. *Mikhail Bakhtin: The Dialogic Principle.* Translated by Wlad Godzich. Minneapolis: University of Minnesota Press, 1984.

Weinstein, James. *The Corporate Ideal in the Liberal State, 1900–1918.* Boston: Beacon Press, 1968.

White, Kevin. *The First Sexual Revolution.* New York: New York University Press, 1993.

Wiebe, Robert H. *The Search for Order: 1877–1920.* New York: Hill and Wang, 1967.

Wiltsher, Anne. *Most Dangerous Women: Feminist Peace Campaigners of the Great War.* Boston: Routledge and Keegan Paul, Pandora Press, 1985.

Wolfe, Donald M. *The Image of Man in America*, 2nd ed. New York: Thomas Y. Crowell Co., 1970.

Wyllie, Irvin G. *The Self-made Man in America: The Myth of Rags to Riches.* New Brunswick, N.J.: Rutgers University Press, 1954.

Wynn, Neil A. *From Progressivism to Prosperity: World War I and American Society.* New York: Holmes and Meier, 1986.

Articles, Essays, and Dissertations

Buenker, John D. "Essay." In *Progressivism*, ed. John D. Buenker, John C. Burnham, and Robert M. Crunden, 31. Cambridge, Mass.: Schenkman, 1977.

Chatfield, Charles. "World War I and the Liberal Pacifist in the United States." *American Historical Review* 61 (December 1970): 1920–1937.

Cook, Blanche Wiesen. "The Woman's Peace Party: Collaboration and Cooperation." *Peace and Change: A Journal of Peace Research* 1, no. 1 (Fall 1972): 36–42.

____. "Woodrow Wilson and the Anti-Militarists, 1914–1918." Ph.D. diss., Johns Hopkins University, 1970.

Cooper, John Milton, Jr. "Progressivism and American Foreign Policy: A Reconsideration." *Mid-America* 51 (October 1969): 260–277.

Dubois, Ellen Carol. "Harriot Stanton Blatch and the Transformation of Class Relations Among Women Suffragists." In *Gender, Class, Race and*

Reform in the Progressive Era, ed. Nancy S. Dye and Noralee Frankel, 162–179. Lexington: University of Kentucky Press, 1991.

Echols, Alice. "'Women Power' and Women's Liberation: Exploring the Relationship Between the Antiwar Movement and the Women's Liberation Movement." In *Give Peace a Chance*, ed. William D. Hoover and Melvin Small, 171–181. Syracuse, N.Y.: Syracuse University Press, 1992.

Filene, Peter. "The World Peace Foundation and Progressivism: 1910–1918." *New England Quarterly* 36 (December 1963): 484–501.

Howlett, Charles R. "Women Pacifists in America: Women's View at the Lake Mohonk Conferences for International Arbitration, 1895–1916." *Peace Research* 21 (January 1989): 27–32, 69–74.

Kennedy, David. "Overview: The Progressive Era." *Historian* 37 (May 1975): 436–452.

Lears, T. J. Jackson. "The Concept of Cultural Hegemony: Problems and Possibilities." *American Historical Review* 90 (June 1985): 567–593.

Lutzker, Michael A. "The Pacifist as Militarist: A Critique of the American Peace Movement, 1898–1914." *Societas* 5 (Spring 1975): 87–104.

Manahan, Nancy. "Future Old Maids and Pacifist Agitators: The Story of Tracy Mygatt and Francis Witherspoon." *Women's Studies Quarterly* 10 (Spring 1982): 10–13.

Martin, James Parker. "The American Peace Movement and the Progressive Era, 1910–1917." Ph.D. diss., Rice University, 1975.

McCormick, Richard L. "The Discovery that 'Business Corrupts Politics': A Reappraisal of Progressivism." *American Historical Review* 86 (1981): 247–274.

McGovern, James R. "David Graham Phillips and the Virility Impulse of Progressives." *New England Quarterly* 39 (September 1966): 334–355.

Nafziger, Ralph O. "The American Press and Public Opinion and the World War, 1914–April, 1917." Ph.D. diss., University of Wisconsin, 1938.

Parsons, Susan F. "Feminism and the Logic of Morality: A Consideration of Alternatives." In *Ethics: A Feminist Reader*, ed. Elizabeth Fraser, Jennifer Hornsby, and Sabina Lovibond, 380–497. Oxford: Blackwell, 1992.

Patterson, David S. "The Emergence of Peace History." *Reviews in American History* 23 (1995): 129–136.

____. "An Interpretation of the American Peace Movement, 1898–1914." In *Peace Movements in America*, ed. Charles Chatfield. New York: Schocken Books, 1973.

Schott, Linda Kay. "The Woman's Peace Party and the Moral Basis for Women's Pacifism." *Frontiers* 7, no. 2 (1985): 18–24.

Scott, Joan W. "Women and War: A Focus for Rewriting History." *Women's Studies Quarterly* 12, no.2 (Summer 1984): 2–13.

Scott, Joan Wallach. "Gender: A Useful Category of Historical Analysis." *American Historical Review* 91 (December 1986): 1053–1075.

Sheppard, Alice. "Political and Social Consciousness in the Woman Suffrage Cartoons of Lou Rogers and Nina Allender." *Studies in American Humor* 4 (Fall 1985): 39–49.

Sicherman, Barbara. "Working It Out: Gender, Profession and Reform in the Career of Alice Hamilton." In *Gender, Class, and Race in the Progressive Era*, ed. Nancy S. Dye and Noralee Frankel, 127–147. Lexington: University of Kentucky Press, 1991.

Smith-Rosenberg, Carroll. "Writing History: Language, Class and Gender." In *Feminist Studies — Critical Studies*, ed. Teresa D'Lauretis, 31–54. Bloomington: Indiana University Press, 1986.

Stam, Robert. "Mikhail Bakhtin and Left Cultural Critique." In *Postmodernism and its Discontents*, ed. E. Ann Kaplan, 116–145. London: Verso, 1988.

Warren, Karen J., and Duane L. Cady. "Feminism and Peace: Seeing Connections." *Hypatia* 9, no. 2 (Spring 1994): 4–20.

Zeiger, Susan. "She Didn't Raise Her Boy to Be a Slacker: Motherhood, Conscription, and the Culture of the First World War." *Feminist Studies* 22 (Spring 1996): 7–39.

Index

ABOUT THE AUTHOR

ERIKA A. KUHLMAN is Adjunct Assistant Professor of History, Idaho State University. Her main area of research has been the American peace movement.

ISBN 0-313-30341-X

EAN

9 780313 303418

HARDCOVER BAR CODE

90000>